Equality and Diversity
in the
Lifelong Learning Sector

Equality and Diversity
in the
Lifelong Learning Sector

Ann Gravells

Susan Simpson

LearningMatters

First published in 2009 by Learning Matters Ltd.

British Library Cataloguing in Publication Data
A CIP record for this book is available from the British Library.

ISBN: 978 1 84445 197 5

Cover design by Topics – The Creative Partnership
Project management by Deer Park Productions, Tavistock, Devon
Typeset by Pantek Arts Ltd, Maidstone, Kent
Printed and bound in Great Britain by Bell & Bain Ltd, Glasgow

Learning Matters Ltd
33 Southernhay East
Exeter EX1 1NX
Tel: 01392 215560
info@learningmatters.co.uk
www.learningmatters.co.uk

CONTENTS

ACKNOWLEDGEMENTS

The authors would like to thank the following for their support and encouragement while writing this book:

Suzanne Blake
Jenny Davis
Peter Frankish
Bob Gravells
Billy Harrison
Gaynor Mount
Julia Morris
Rachel Simpson
Clare Weaver

The learners and staff of the teacher/training department at Bishop Burton College, and North East Lincolnshire Council Adult Community Learning Service in Grimsby.

The authors and publisher would like to thank the following for permission to reproduce copyright material:

Lifelong Learning UK

Ann Gravells is a lecturer in teacher training at Bishop Burton College in East Yorkshire. She has 24 years' experience of teaching in post-16 education.

She is a consultant to City & Guilds for various projects as well as externally verifying the City & Guilds teacher training qualifications. She has developed International Qualifications in Teaching and Training in Hong Kong, India and Sri Lanka.

Ann holds a Masters in Educational Management, a PGCE, a degree in Education, and a City & Guilds Medal of Excellence for teaching. She is the author of *Preparing to Teach in the Lifelong Learning Sector, Principles and Practice of Assessment in the Lifelong Learning Sector* and co-author of *Planning and Enabling Learning in the Lifelong Learning Sector*. Ann is a Fellow of the Institute for Learning.

Susan Simpson is a teacher in teacher training at the North East Lincolnshire Council's Adult Community Learning Service in Grimsby. She has 25 years' experience of teaching in compulsory and post-16 education.

She is a curriculum manager for education and training, ICT, business administration, and law. She developed, managed and taught adult education programmes in Botswana for ten years. Susan has also presented at regional level for teacher training and nationally for ICT Skills for Life.

Susan holds a postgraduate Diploma in Management Studies, BA (Hons) in Further Education and Training, and Certificate in Education (Hons) in Business Studies and Economics.

The authors welcome any comments from readers; please e-mail consult@ann gravells.co.uk

In this chapter you will learn about:

- the structure of the book and how to use it;
- Lifelong Learning professional teaching standards;
- meanings and benefits of equality and diversity.

The structure of the book and how to use it

This book has been specifically written for those working towards the:

- Certificate in Teaching in the Lifelong Learning Sector (CTLLS);
- Diploma in Teaching in the Lifelong Learning Sector (DTLLS);
- Award in Preparing to Support Learners;
- Certificate in Learning Support.

Equality and Diversity is an optional unit of these qualifications; however, the content is applicable to anyone requiring further information to assist their teaching in an educational context, or for continuing professional development (CPD).

The book is structured in chapters which relate to the content of the *Equality and Diversity* unit. You can work logically through the book or just look up relevant aspects within the chapters which relate to areas of your teaching.

There are activities to enable you to think about how you integrate equality and diversity into your teaching and support, and examples to help you understand the subject. Chapter 6 addresses most of the legislation, employment regulations, policies and codes of practice relevant to the promotion of equality and valuing of diversity. All legislation is subject to change; therefore you are advised to check for any relevant updates or amendments.

At the end of each chapter is a reference and further information list, enabling you to research relevant topics further, by using textbooks, publications and/or the internet. Each chapter is cross-referenced to the new overarching professional standards for teachers, tutors and trainers in the Lifelong Learning Sector.

Throughout this book, the generic term 'teacher' is used, and includes references to learning support practitioners.

The appendices contain a useful list of relevant abbreviations and acronyms, a glossary of terms, the equality and diversity qualification criteria, a checklist for promoting equality and diversity, and sample pro-formas.

The index will help you quickly locate useful topics.

Lifelong Learning professional teaching standards

In September 2007, standards came into effect for all new teachers in the Lifelong Learning Sector who teach on government-funded programmes in England. This includes all post-16 education, including further education, adult and community learning, work based learning and offender education.

Teachers in the Lifelong Learning Sector should value all learners individually and equally. As a teacher, or learning support practitioner, you should be committed to lifelong learning and professional development, and strive for continuous improvement through reflective practice. The key purpose of being a teacher is to create effective and stimulating opportunities for learning, through high-quality teaching that enables the development and progression of all learners.

The full standards encompass six domains:

A   Professional values and practice;
B   Learning and teaching;
C   Specialist learning and teaching;
D   Planning for learning;
E   Assessment for learning;
F   Access and progression.

The standards can be accessed via the Lifelong Learning UK (LLUK) website: www.lluk.org.uk/documents/professional_standards_for_itts_020107.pdf.

If you are taking one of the teaching qualifications, you will need to meet all the relevant criteria relating to the *scope*, *knowledge* and *practice* required in your job role (referenced by: S for *scope*, K for *knowledge* or P for *practice* within the chapters). Level 4 qualifications require academic writing and research skills, and you would need to reference your work to other sources besides this text.

The new qualifications have been developed based upon the Qualifications and Credit Framework (QCF) model, which has mandatory and optional units of assessment at different levels, and different credit values. The units and credits can be built up to form relevant qualifications over time. Equality and Diversity is a six credit unit at level 3 or level 4 and can be found in Appendix 3.

The QCF is currently being phased in (England, Wales and Northern Ireland) and has nine levels: entry, plus 1 to 8. The framework helps learners compare the requirements at each level, and identify a suitable progression route.

Each unit has a credit value which represents ten hours, showing how much time it takes to complete a unit. There are three sizes of qualifications:

- awards (1 to 12 credits);

- certificates (13 to 36 credits);

- diplomas (37 credits or more).

By looking at the title and level of a unit or qualification, learners will be able to see how difficult it is and how long it will take to complete. A comparison of the levels to existing qualifications is:

- level 1 – GCSEs (grades D–G);

- level 2 – GCSEs (grade A*–C);

- level 3 – A levels;

- level 4 – foundation degree;

- level 5 – degree;

- level 6 – honours degree;

- level 7 – masters degree;

- level 8 – doctor of philosophy (PhD).

Further information regarding qualifications and levels can be found at the direct.gov website via the internet shortcut http://tinyurl.com/66ftqx.

Depending upon whether you are a teacher or learning support practitioner, you will need to take the qualification which is relevant to your role. Further details regarding these can be located via the Lifelong Learning website (www.lluk.org.uk).

All teachers must register with the Institute for Learning (IfL), the professional body for teachers, trainers, tutors and trainee teachers in the learning and skills sector, and maintain their continuing professional development (CPD). Once registered, they must abide by their Code of Professional Practice; further details can be found via their website (www.ifl.ac.uk).

Registering with the IfL, gaining the relevant qualification, and maintaining your CPD, will enable you to apply for your teaching status. This will be either: Associate Teacher Learning and Skills (ATLS) for *associate* teachers, or Qualified Teacher Learning and Skills (QTLS) for *full* teachers. This is a requirement under the Further Education Teachers' Qualifications (England) Regulations (2007). Further details regarding the associate and full teaching roles can be found via the IfL website.

Meanings and benefits of equality and diversity

To effectively promote equality and diversity, it is important you understand some of the terminology used. In Appendix 2, you will find a glossary of terms which will prove a valuable starting point for your knowledge, and a useful reference.

There are six strands of equality. These are:

- age;
- disability;
- gender;
- race;
- religion and belief;
- sexual orientation.

They are covered by legislative foundations, further details of which can be found in Chapter 6.

The changing and diverse nature of society poses many challenges for individuals, groups, employers and teachers. To effectively promote the inclusion of all people in society, there is a need to bring equality, diversity and rights issues into the main-stream, to ensure they are no longer viewed as something affecting only minority groups. Those affected by stereotyping, prejudice and discrimination are not always in the minority. The government White Paper *Fairness for all* (DTI, May 2004) noted that 8 per cent of the UK population are from different ethnic backgrounds and 22 per cent are disabled adults. Add to this the number of people who have been affected by prejudice and discrimination, for example, age, religion, sex and sexual orientation, and you can see that many individuals could be the subject of unfair treatment. This could be at some point in their lives, whether in education, employment or accessing goods and services. Having organisational policies, procedures and codes of practice, and following government legislation will help you promote a more inclusive learning environment.

When teaching, you may have a group of learners from different backgrounds and cultures, and/or with different needs and abilities. You can add value to your teaching by recognising the many differences your learners have, and incorporating their diverse experiences into your sessions. By combating discrimination, valuing diversity and promoting equality, you should be able to create a positive and equal learning environment. You can help ensure your learners are motivated and comfortable in their environment by being positive, considerate and respectful, and by doing so, encourage these qualities in your learners and colleagues. If you have a learner with a disability, don't label them as *disabled* but consider them as an individual with a variation in ability. These variations are what make your learners unique, and they shouldn't be excluded from the learning process as a result. Everyone is different in some way from others, and these differences should be celebrated and acknowledged to give equal opportunities to all.

Equality is about the rights of learners to have access to, attend and participate in their chosen learning experience. This should be regardless of ability and/or circumstances. Inequality and discrimination should be tackled to ensure fairness, decency and respect among learners. Equal opportunity is a concept underpinned by legislation to provide relevant and appropriate access for the participation, development and advancement of all individuals and groups.

In the past, equality has often been described as *everyone being the same* or *having the same opportunities*. Nowadays, it can be described as *everyone being different, but having equal rights*.

Diversity is about valuing and respecting the differences in learners, regardless of ability and/or circumstances, or any other individual characteristics they may have. If you have two or more learners, you will experience diversity. You are also different from your learners in many ways, and they are different from one another, therefore they are entitled to be treated with respect, with their differences taken into consideration.

Skills for Business state:

> Combined together, equality and diversity drive an organisation to comply with anti-discrimination legislation as well as emphasising the positive benefits of diversity such as drawing on a wider pool of talent, positively motivating all employees and meeting the needs of a wider customer base.
>
> (www.sfbn-equality-diversity.org.uk/meaning.html)

Differences should be acknowledged, celebrated and embraced, to ensure all learners feel included in the learning process, and the learning environment is suitable for all.

Examples of these differences are:

- ability
- age
- belief
- colour
- class
- clothing worn
- confidence
- culture

- disability – physical or mental
- domestic circumstances
- educational background
- employment status
- ethnic origin
- experience
- gender
- intelligence

- language, accent, dialect
- learning difficulties
- marital status/civil partnership
- nationality
- occupation
- parental status
- physical characteristics
- political conviction
- race
- religion
- sexual orientation
- social class or identity
- talent
- tradition
- transgender
- wealth

The chapters in this book will help you to understand how to promote equality and diversity within your teaching and learning environment. The benefits of implementing this will help ensure:

- a better understanding of religions, faiths and cultures;
- a climate of trust, respect and tolerance towards others;
- a positive learning experience for all;
- achievement of learning goals;
- assessment is fair;
- communication is open and honest;
- learners are content and happy;
- diversity is recognised and celebrated;
- effective teamwork;
- improved working relationships;
- motivation is increased;
- individual needs are met;
- resources do not discriminate against anyone;
- sessions can be planned to relate to all interests, abilities and cultures;
- stereotyping, prejudice and discrimination do not take place.

Lifelong Learning UK is committed to, and actively promotes, equality and diversity in the sector:

> Promoting diversity in the lifelong learning workforce is about attracting and retaining the best people, regardless of what group they belong to. There is considerable evidence to show that inclusive organisations benefit from diversity through:
>
> - enhanced competitiveness – attracting and retaining more competent employees, who understand the needs of their learners and respect differences;

- *improved performance and outcomes – creating a working environment in which everyone is encouraged to perform to their maximum potential;*

- *improved customer services – being able to reflect and meet the diverse needs of learners and;*

- *improved staff relations, which reduce the risk of costly tribunals by complying with anti-discriminatory legislation.*

(www.lluk.org.uk/3167.htm)

As a teacher working in the Lifelong Learning Sector, you should agree with the above statement, particularly *creating a working environment in which everyone is encouraged to perform to their maximum potential.* An inclusive organisation will ensure learners are not excluded for any reason, either directly or indirectly, from partaking in their chosen programme. All your learners will bring with them valuable skills, knowledge and experiences; try to incorporate these within your sessions, and treat everyone as an individual. You should be positive and proactive where equality and diversity are concerned, even if your own opinions differ from those of your learners. You may have to challenge your own values and beliefs. However, as a professional, you are first and foremost a teacher, and your personal opinions must not interfere with the teaching and learning process. You must also be careful not to indulge the minority to the detriment of the majority.

If you ever feel unsure as to whether you, or other learners and colleagues, are valuing equality and diversity, just ask yourself *is this fair?*, or, *how would I feel in this situation?* or *would I want to be treated in this way?* If your answer is a negative one, then make sure you do something about it.

The Learning and Skills Council (LSC) exists to make England better skilled and more competitive. Their vision is that:

> *By 2010, young people and adults in England will have knowledge and skills matching the best in the world and be part of a truly competitive workforce. We are sure this vision can be achieved through a strong commitment to equality and diversity.*
> (www.lsc.gov.uk/aboutus/equality-diversity/)

You will probably be teaching on programmes funded by the LSC, and therefore will be able to contribute towards their vision by your own commitment to equality and diversity within your organisation.

A report by Her Majesty's Inspectorate (HMI), *Race equality in further education* (2005), found:

> *The promotion of equality and diversity through the curriculum is a common feature, but it is rarely embedded consistently across the whole curriculum.*

As a teacher, you need to ensure you are embedding all aspects of equality and diversity within the curriculum you are responsible for. You may be inspected at some time and will need to demonstrate how you are embedding these into your teaching. An example of promoting equality could start with the way your organisation advertises their programmes, to ensure they are promoting accessibility for all prospective learners. This would then follow through the recruitment and interviewing stages, induction, initial assessment, teaching, assessment and evaluation. Always include your learners in relevant activities and the full learning process, rather than excluding anyone for any reason. The best way to ensure you are effectively including all learners, and treating them equally, is to ask them if there is anything you can do to help, or that can be done differently for them. To value and promote diversity among your learners, you need to embrace their differences, and encourage interaction and support, challenging any negative beliefs.

Equal opportunities is defined by the Scotland Act 1998 as:

> ...the prevention, elimination or regulation of discrimination between persons on grounds of sex or marital status, on racial grounds, or on grounds of disability, age, sexual orientation, language or social origin, or of other personal attributes, including beliefs or opinions, such as religious beliefs or political opinions.

Depending upon the nation within which you are employed, there may be different definitions; however, you should always treat others with respect and understanding.

An interesting quote way ahead of its time is from Aristotle (384–322 BC): *It is as unfair to treat unequals equally, as equals unequally.* Always treat your learners and colleagues fairly, with dignity and respect, just as you would wish to be treated. Try to become familiar with the specific customs or needs that a learner's faith or culture might have. This will ensure you are promoting equality and diversity as part of your everyday teaching, and including rather than excluding learners.

The Royal Mail Group has a comprehensive website with a very useful interactive diversity quiz regarding culture and religion. You might like to use it to test your own knowledge, or to create a discussion with your learners. It can be accessed at http://tinyurl.com/3pt7b5.

Summary

In this chapter you have learnt about:

- the structure of the book and how to use it;
- Lifelong Learning professional teaching standards;
- meanings and benefits of equality and diversity.

References and further information

Daniels, K and MacDonald, L (2005) *Equality, diversity and discrimination.* Chartered Institute of Personnel and Development

Gravells, A (2008) *Preparing to teach in the Lifelong Learning Sector* (3rd edn). Exeter: Learning Matters

Gravells, A and Simpson, S (2008) *Planning and enabling learning.* Exeter: Learning Matters

HMI Report (2005) *Race equality in further education: progress and good practice in colleges in the further education sector.* HMI 2463

LLUK (2006) *New overarching professional standards for teachers, tutors and trainers in the Lifelong Learning Sector.* London: LLUK

Spencer, L (2005) *Diversity pocketbook.* Alresford Management Pocketbooks Ltd

White, L and Weaver, S (2007) *Curriculum for diversity guide.* Leicester: NIACE

Websites

Equality and Diversity Forum – www.edf.org.uk

Equality and Human Rights Commission – www.equalityhumanrights.com

Further Education Teachers' Qualifications (England) Regulations (2007) – www.legislation.gov.uk/si/si2007/20072264.htm

Institute for Learning – www.ifl.ac.uk

Lifelong Learning UK – www.lluk.org.uk

Learning and Skills Council – www.lsc.gov.uk

National Institute for Adult Continuing Education – www.niace.org.uk

Skills for Business Equality and Diversity – www.sfbn-equality-diversity.org.uk/Index.htm

Royal Mail Group – www.royalmailgroup.com

1 KEY FEATURES OF A CULTURE THAT PROMOTES EQUALITY AND VALUES DIVERSITY

Introduction

In this chapter you will learn about:

- promoting a positive culture;

- grievances, complaints and appeals.

There are activities and examples to help you reflect on the above which will assist your understanding of the key features of a culture which promotes equality and diversity.

You may like to refer to Appendix 2 for the glossary of terms. This will help your knowledge and understanding of the various terms used throughout this chapter.

This chapter contributes towards the following: scope (S), knowledge (K) and practice (P) aspects of the professional standards (A–F domains) for teachers, tutors and trainers in the Lifelong Learning Sector:

AS1, AS2, AS3, AS4, AS5, AS6, AS7;
AK1.1, AK2.1, AK2.2, AK3.1 AK4.2, AK5.1, AK5.2, AK6.1, AK6.2;
AP1.1, AP2.1, AP2.2, AP3.1, AP5.1, AP5.2, AP6.1, AP6.2, AP7.1;
BS1, BS2, BS3, BS4;
BK1.1, BK1.2, BK1.3, BK2.2, BK2.5, BK3.4;
BP1.1, BP1.2, BP2.5;
DS1;
DK1.1;
DP1.1, DP1.3;
FS1, FS2;
FK1.1, FK1.2, FK4.1, FK4.2;
FP1.2, FP4.1.

The standards can be accessed at:
www.lluk.org.uk/documents/professional_standards_for_itts_020107.pdf.

Promoting a positive culture

As a professional teacher in a diverse and multicultural society, you need to help promote a positive culture within your teaching and learning environment. Think of culture as the way of life, or the way things are done within your organisation. It's the beliefs and customs of a particular group of people, for example those you work with. If you feel your organisation isn't very proactive promoting a positive culture, there's no reason to be complacent; you can do things yourself to ensure your learners are all treated fairly. You may need to challenge your own attitudes, values and beliefs, to accept and respect others. If other people see your positive attitude and the proactive ways you embrace equality and diversity with your learners, this may help improve the culture of your organisation. While working towards the teaching standards, you will need to:

> *Establish a purposeful learning environment where learners feel safe, secure, confident and valued (BP1.1).*

> *Establish and maintain procedures with learners which promote and maintain appropriate behaviour, communication and respect for others, while challenging discriminatory behaviour and attitudes. (BP1.2)*

> (LLUK, 2007)

To help achieve this, and to ensure your learners have an equal and fair chance with their education, you need to recognise that people are different. This can be the way they look, behave, dress, their beliefs, and/or where they live and work, their background, culture, gender and age. In a diverse and multicultural society, recognising and accepting individual differences are part of embracing equality and diversity.

Sometimes, assumptions are made about people because of how they look or act. This might be deliberate on their part to fit in with a particular group, for fear of discrimination. As a teacher, you need to get to know your learners as individuals, to encourage them to be themselves and to promote an inclusive culture within your groups. This can lead to greater confidence and a sense of belonging on the learner's part, better communication within the group and respect for individual differences. To create an inclusive environment, you should involve all your learners during your sessions, and not exclude anyone for any reason, either directly or indirectly. All learners have the right to be valued as individuals, and are entitled to attend and participate in their chosen programme. You should differentiate your approach and resources to meet any individual needs.

> *A curriculum offer should have something for everyone and be as inclusive as possible in order to ensure that as wide a range of learners as possible can take advantage of it... A curriculum for diversity should encompass everything that a provider has to offer, including what is taught, who teaches it, what is known and expected of learners, as well as where learning takes place. It is a perspective on adult education that should permeate everything.*

> (White and Weaver, 2007, ix)

You might not be in a position to design various aspects of the curriculum, but as a teacher, you are responsible for groups and/or individuals you teach, and the experiences they have while they are with you. To help benefit your learners, you need to familiarise yourself with the diverse nature of today's society and cultures, to be able to offer equal experiences to all your learners.

Activity

Find out what you can about the various beliefs, faiths and religions in our society (for example, agnosticism, atheism, Buddhism, Christianity, Hinduism, Islam, Jehovah's Witness, Judaism, Mormon, Paganism, Rastafarianism, Shinto, Sikhism, Taoism, etc). Having some knowledge of these will help you understand and appreciate the diverse nature of others.

There are many individual and social factors, besides those mentioned already, that should be taken into consideration. These can encompass physical, mental and emotional characteristics; likes and dislikes; attitudes, values and beliefs; personality traits; politics, morals and ethics; type of household; social identity; clothing worn; and past experiences. People naturally have perceptions about others, which can often be wrong; therefore information and knowledge can help change how your learners perceive one another. Becoming knowledgeable of how you can support your learners to embrace their differences will help create a more confident learner with a sense of belonging. If ever you are unsure how to help a particular learner, just ask them. However, try not to embarrass them in front of their peers.

The Centre for Excellence in Leadership (2005, 5) states:

> People are diverse in the way they learn. Learning approaches may be inherent, but may also be shaped by cultural experience. The greater the variety of experiences a learning group may have at its disposal, the greater the capacity for thinking differently and problem-solving in innovative ways. There are a high number of learners from minority groups in the learning and skills sector. For providers, there are challenges in engaging those learners and keeping them on track and this is exacerbated by issues such as institutional discrimination. An organisational culture which encourages diversity and provides culturally relevant role models creates a more representative learning environment, and leads to better results.

Hopefully, your organisation will embrace the above statement, and you are working within a culture which promotes positive learning approaches. If not, you may need to encourage change, within yourself and your learners, as a start.

Learners may have attitudes, values and beliefs which they have inherited from others, without having the opportunity to develop their own. These could include set ways of thinking, or preconceived ideas of other cultures that are not based on fact. Ignorance should be no excuse for treating someone unfairly; however, part of your role should be to encourage a climate of acceptance and support, informed by fact, and not based upon a person's background, upbringing, culture or religion, etc. Your learners need to accept they may have different attitudes, values and beliefs to those of other learners, but that these should not interfere with the group cohesion or learning process. Indeed, you may feel differently about certain issues, and you don't have to necessarily believe or agree with all your learners, but you must not let your opinions interfere with the teaching and learning process. You must also be careful not to be biased in any way towards a particular type of group or learner.

More Eastern European countries have now joined the European Union, increasing immigration to the United Kingdom (UK) and many of these people will have English as a second language. Society is changing and people are now more tolerant towards different cultures and traditions. Having a positive attitude in front of others, including all learners in activities, and encouraging a professional working relationship amongst everyone, will help promote an understanding and tolerant climate during your sessions. If your learners and colleagues see your positive and proactive attitude, it will help them adopt the same, therefore changing the culture.

Activity

Find out who is responsible for equality and diversity within your organisation, and whether any training is available which you could attend.

To ensure equality and diversity is no longer viewed as something only affecting minority groups, any issues need to be viewed not as issues, but as something to be explored and celebrated. Learners could be personally affected by stereotyping, prejudice and/or discrimination when attending sessions – for example, their disability, age, religion or sexual orientation, which could lead to non-attendance or non-achievement. As a teacher, you need to ensure all your learners value one another and that the basic rights they are entitled to, for example, to learn in an comfortable and safe environment, are met.

The induction to your organisation should have included details of all policies and procedures, including equality and diversity. You should also bring these to the attention of your learners, perhaps during their initial interview or induction session. However, having a policy is not enough: there should be a working group or committee to ensure it is promoted, monitored and regularly reviewed.

Example

The organisation fully supports all principles of equality and diversity, and opposes any unfair or unlawful discrimination on the grounds of ability, age, colour, culture, disability, domestic circumstances, employment status, ethnic origin, gender, learning difficulties, marital status/civil partnership, nationality, political conviction, race, religion or belief, sexual orientation and/or social background.

The organisation aims to ensure that equality and diversity is promoted among all staff and learners, and that unfair or unlawful discrimination, whether direct or indirect, is eliminated to promote a climate of equality and respect. All staff and learners can expect to work in an environment free from harassment and bullying.

Combined, equality and diversity will drive your organisation to comply with anti-discrimination legislation, as well as emphasising the positive benefits. This includes embracing learner experiences, cultures and differences, while enabling each individual's maximum potential to be fulfilled.

Activity

Locate the equality and diversity policy within your organisation. Have a look at it and compare it with the one in the example on page 13. Would you recommend any changes to it, or do you feel it's acceptable?

If you had difficulty locating the policy, your learners may also have difficulty. It could be that it's called something else, for example, an *Equal Opportunities Policy*. Having looked at it, would you know what to do if you, or a learner, had a problem, or do you feel you would like to be a part of the working group or committee? Usually, a policy will be accompanied by a procedure that may be located elsewhere. This will state the process that should be gone through if there is a problem or complaint, and what will be done about it, within specific timeframes.

To help promote equality and diversity, organisations should ensure:

- a wide range of relevant services are available to support learning;
- awareness is raised through relevant training;
- barriers to participation are removed;
- equality and diversity are reflected in the recruitment and selection of staff and learners;
- problems and complaints are followed up by the working group or committee;
- staff and learners are supported as necessary;
- staff are aware of the diverse nature of today's society;
- staff are familiar with current legislation;
- the teaching environment and resources are appropriate, fair and inclusive;
- they have a current and relevant policy which is promoted, monitored and regularly reviewed.

The policy should be regularly monitored, for example, gathering information and data to support any problems or complaints, ensuring there is no unintentional discrimination, and keeping track of recruitment, training and development. The policy should also be reviewed in the light of any legislative changes, or organisational amendments. Having a policy often leads to a reactive situation, where problems are dealt with afterwards. However, it's best to be proactive and stop problems occurring in the first place. Policies should be designed to prevent or respond to events or problems.

Example

Binder's college is hoping to recruit another female to the computing department; there are currently seven males and only one female. The senior management think they will be exempt from the Sex Discrimination Act to address the balance of males and females. They ask the Equality and Diversity working group to look at their advertisement, who advises it is illegal to advertise purely for a female.

It is not acceptable to discriminate in favour of a particular group, for example, females. In this example, the senior management should look at their recruitment and selection procedures to ensure that they are not discriminating, and will employ the right person for the job. The law does allow for organisations to encourage applications from under-represented groups, but does not allow for selection to be made simply on the basis of race or sex. The only time that you can discriminate in favour of a particular sex is if it is a genuine occupational qualification (GOQ) for a particular job, for example, if it is restricted to one sex as it requires living in single-sex accommodation, or is in a single-sex establishment.

Activity

Do you feel you have discriminated against anyone you work with, or a learner, intentionally or not? Think about how you act in the staff room at break times, how you communicate with your colleagues and learners, and the types of resources you use when teaching. Do you have a positive attitude or do you feel you have been influenced by others?

It could be that you follow what other people do, rather than making your own decisions regarding your attitudes, values and beliefs. When teaching, you should build up a climate of trust, openness and honesty with your colleagues and learners, and encourage them to integrate and treat one another with respect. Learners should be supported to achieve their maximum potential without making them feel excluded or discriminated against – for example, needing time to attend a religious or cultural event. Initial assessment will help obtain any specific information regarding individual learners that may need to be addressed. Knowledge of dates of relevant religious festivals, etc., that may impact upon your teaching sessions will help when planning your scheme of work. However, legislation does not dictate when holidays must be taken, and nobody is entitled to more holiday than others because of their religion or ethnic origin.

Grievances, complaints and appeals

At some point during the teaching and learning process, one of your learners may have a grievance, a complaint or even wish to appeal against one of your decisions. They will need to know who they can go to, and that the issue will be followed up.

You may also have a grievance yourself and need to know what to do. Organisations should have relevant policies and procedures in place. A policy states what the organisation's commitment is, a procedure states how the policy will be implemented. There may be separate policies and procedures for staff and for learners, which may be available in handbooks, given during induction, on a notice board, or available via your organisation's intranet. Make sure you are familiar with these; they will usually be reviewed yearly, and should be dated to ensure their currency. There should be a grievance, complaints and appeals procedure, for staff and for learners; they may be separate, or integrated into one.

Activity

Locate your organisation's policies and procedures for grievances, complaints and appeals (for staff and for learners). See when these were last reviewed and who is responsible for them.

You may have found there is one policy for all three aspects, with separate procedures for staff and learners for each. Reading them will ensure you are familiar with what to do in case any problems arise.

An organisational positive and proactive culture towards equality and diversity should help reduce the numbers of grievances, complaints and appeals. This can be achieved by all staff within the organisation, taking issues seriously and partaking in training to increase their awareness. You also need to know that your own behaviour can impact on your organisation's culture: being negative may only breed negativity among others. Being positive should influence others to be positive too.

Sometimes learners may have a grievance, but not bring this to your attention for fear of it being seen as an over-reaction, or that the issue might become worse as a result. It's important to watch what's happening during your sessions. If you see a learner acting withdrawn, or not wanting to sit next to someone or work with another particular learner, have an informal chat with them to see if you can help in any way.

Example

Ninghong commenced a Customer Service programme at the same time as 15 other learners. Her English was quite good, but she always sat on her own and didn't want to work in a group. Her teacher asked her during the lunch break if anything was wrong. She confided she felt the others were making fun of her name and culture, but didn't want to make a formal complaint. Her teacher amended the next session to include greeting visitors from other countries, and used various activities to bring an awareness of other cultures to the group. The group were not aware this was a direct result of Ninghong's chat with her teacher. Afterwards, Ninghong felt more included in the group, and several learners were showing an interest and asking her for more information about her culture.

Grievances and complaints can often be dealt with informally, without the perpetrators knowing. However, if you feel a problem is more serious, your organisation's procedure should always be followed, as legal rights may be lost if not.

Example

Greg is a teacher at your organisation, and confides in you that he is gay. He tells you he feels he didn't get a promotion because of this and has therefore been discriminated against. You encourage him to follow the organisation's complaints procedure, but he doesn't want to make a fuss. You tell him that it doesn't have to be him that makes the complaint, but that you could raise a grievance about discrimination within the organisation. He doesn't want you to do this either. It could be that Greg didn't get the promotion because of his ability, not because he is gay. Greg should really have an informal chat with his manager to gain some feedback regarding his interview. He can then make a decision whether his complaint is valid. If it is, following the organisation's procedure will ensure everything is documented, in case a tribunal is involved at some stage in the future.

If you raise a grievance about discrimination, it is against the law for your organisation to treat you badly as a result, as this is victimisation, whether it relates to you or to someone else. It is also against the law to be treated badly for supporting someone else's complaint about discrimination, for example, by giving evidence to support their grievance.

The grievance or complaints procedure should not be used just to get back at someone because you are annoyed with something they have done or said. If you feel that you have been unfairly treated, and your complaint is genuine, then don't wait too long. Anyone following up your complaint will wonder why you hadn't complained about it before, and that could weaken your case. The same will apply to your learners, if you feel they have a valid complaint: encourage them to follow the procedure; don't wait for things to get worse if you can't resolve the issue informally.

Example

Learner grievance and complaints procedure

Any grievance or complaint should be made in writing to the Learner Services Manager, clearly setting out the problem. A written response will be made within seven days, along with an invitation to a meeting to discuss the problem. A parent, carer or other representative may be present at the meeting. Within a further seven days, a written decision will be made. An appeal can be made against this decision within 14 days.

Some organisations will provide a pro-forma for learners to use for their grievance or complaint, which ensures all the required details are obtained, or will encourage an informal discussion prior to a formal complaint. Statistics should be maintained regarding all grievances and complaints, which will help the organisation when reviewing their policies and procedures. An anonymous suggestion box can often be a way to encourage learners to express their concerns in confidence. This way, your organisation can be proactive regarding potential problems, rather than being reactive afterwards.

Setting ground rules at the commencement of a programme can help promote a climate of respect among learners; ensuring boundaries are set and followed by all. Role-play activities can be a way to bring an awareness of harassment or bullying to your group. During tutorial sessions with your learners, you could note any problems on your tutorial review forms; this would ensure a formal record.

Most organisations now have a policy for harassment and bullying; find out if there is one available for your learners, and ensure they are aware of it.

Example

Harassment and bullying policy

This organisation is committed to promoting a positive environment where all staff and learners can expect to be treated with dignity and respect. Staff and learners have the right to work in a climate free from harassment and bullying. If an issue cannot be dealt with informally, the grievance and complaints procedure should be followed. All complaints will be taken seriously and investigated fully, with appropriate action being taken as a result.

Harassment and bullying can take many forms, including name-calling, physical or mental abuse, offensive or insulting jokes or literature, derogatory or rude comments, ignoring others or undermining someone's confidence. As a result, morale can be lowered, stress, anxiety and harm caused, and ill health and poor performance can occur. Harassment is a disciplinary offence and may be illegal. You might be able to deal with some problems informally; however, if you have any cause for concern, always take this further before it gets out of control. Once you have reported a problem, your organisation must follow this up and do all they reasonably can to put a stop to it.

As part of your teaching role, you may be assessing your learners, marking tests and assignments, etc. Your judgements may affect your learners' future career prospects, and they have a right to appeal against your decision, and your organisation should have a learner appeals procedure, outlining the stages involved. The appeals procedure should be available to learners when they commence the programme and you should familiarise yourself with it.

Example

Learner appeals procedure

Stage one – within seven days of receiving the assessment decision, discuss the issue with the assessor concerned, to clarify the reasons for the grade.

Stage two – if the issue has not been resolved, put this in writing to the internal verifier, or programme manager, within seven days. This may result in a reassessment of your work. A response will be made within 14 days.

Stage three – if the issue has still not been resolved, put this in writing to the Learner Services Manager within seven days, who will respond within 14 days.

Stage four – if you are still not happy, you can request your appeal be heard by the Appeals Panel, at their next meeting, who may inform the Awarding/Examining or External body responsible for your qualification. Their decision will be final.

If the programme you teach and assess is externally moderated or verified, i.e. a representative from the Awarding/Examining body visits to ensure compliance with their regulations, they will ask to see records of any appeals. They may also talk to your learners to ensure they have received a fair learning and assessment process. The National Vocational Qualification (NVQ) Code of Practice states: *Awarding bodies must take account of current legislation in the area of access to fair assessment and equal opportunities (2006, 4).*

Example

Cheryl was working towards the National Vocational Qualification (NVQ) in hairdressing at level 3. She had been observed in the workplace by her supervisor, who had said she wasn't yet competent at one of the units, but Cheryl felt she was. When the external verifier visited, he asked her if she had registered a formal appeal. Cheryl said she hadn't, but had discussed it with her assessor at the college, who had arranged to go into her workplace to carry out an observation the following week. The external verifier clarified this with the assessor, who confirmed Cheryl's supervisor was not a qualified assessor and could not make the final decision.

If any of your learners do have a grievance, complaint or appeal, this should not affect the way you, or other learners or staff, treat them. You should always remain professional in your role, to promote a positive learning environment.

Summary

In this chapter you have learnt about:

- promoting a positive culture;

- grievances, complaints and appeals.

References and further information

CEL (2005) *Leading change in equality and diversity – the Centre for Excellence in Leadership's Strategy for Improving Diversity in Leadership in the Learning and Skills Sector.* London: CEL

DTI (2006) *Work and families: choice and flexibility.* Department of Trade and Industry 06/707

HMI (2006) *Working together to safeguard children: a guide to inter-agency working to safeguard and promote the welfare of children.* HM Government

LLUK (2007) *New Overarching Professional Teaching Standards.* London: LLUK

Learning and Skills Council (2007) *Equality and diversity – what's that then?* East Midlands: LSC

NVQ Code of Practice (2006). London: QCA

Press for Change (2007) *Guidance on trans equality in post school education.* London: Unison

White, L and Weaver, S (2007) *Curriculum for diversity guide.* Leicester: NIACE

Websites

Advice Services Alliance – www.advicenow.org.uk/grievances

Employment Tribunals Online – www.employmenttribunals.gov.uk

Equality for Lesbians, Gay Men and Bisexuals – www.stonewall.org.uk

Every Child Matters – www.everychildmatters.gov.uk

Immigration Advisory Service – www.ias.uk.org

Mental health – www.mind.org.uk

Workplace bullying – www.workplacebullying.co.uk

Introduction

> In this chapter you will learn about:
>
> - applying and promoting the principles of equality and diversity;
> - promotion of equality;
> - benefits of diversity.

There are activities and examples to help you reflect on the above which will assist your understanding of how to promote equality and value diversity.

The appendices contain useful pro-formas you may wish to use.

This chapter contributes towards the following: scope (S), knowledge (K) and practice (P) aspects of the professional standards (A–F domains) for teachers, tutors and trainers in the Lifelong Learning Sector:

AS3;
AK3.1;
AP3.1;
BS1, BS5;
BK1.2, BK5.2;
BP1.2, BP5.2;
DS1;
DK1.1;
DP1.1;
ES2;
EK2.1;
EP2.1.

The standards can be accessed at:
www.lluk.org.uk/documents/professional_standards_for_itts_020107.pdf.

Applying and promoting the principles of equality and diversity

When applying and promoting the principles of equality and diversity in your teaching practice there are many legal, statutory and inspection frameworks that you need to be aware of which will affect your programme planning and behaviour towards your learners.

Legislation requires organisations to examine their functions, frameworks, services, policies and procedures. They are required to assess whether they could, or do, have a negative impact on people from particular groups who may have been excluded or discriminated against, for example, having an appropriate physical environment which can be accessed by all learners. It is also important for organisations to examine if their actions have a positive impact on promoting equality, and to share that good practice within the wider organisation as well as externally with other agencies.

Inspection bodies, for example, the Office for Standards in Education, Children's Services and Skills (Ofsted). The requirements of inspection bodies should translate into a key strategic aim for your organisation with an action plan which is rigorously monitored. Very clear guidelines should be developed for teachers, setting out what is expected of them and where to go for specialist advice. All staff in your organisation should receive equality and diversity training, and understand how to reduce barriers to avoid harassment, victimisation and discrimination against people within the six strands, and how to respond to safeguarding requirements when teaching vulnerable adults.

As a teacher, it is likely that you will have come across many constraints and barriers that exist for your learners. Your expertise in your subject knowledge and practical skills, as well as diverse work experience, may have been the starting point for your entry to teaching. You are also an employee and more than likely belong to a diverse workforce, particularly where there is an attempt by organisations to represent all areas. Building your teaching practice on a variety of life and work experiences is a good basis for a common-sense approach to equality and diversity. However, responsibility for promoting and applying equality and diversity in an integrated way, and taking account of the needs of all learners, is being driven at various levels within society. According to Barbara Roche, former Minister for Women:

> The Government's vision is of an equal, inclusive society is where everyone is treated with respect and where there is opportunity for all. Everyone needs to be able to play their full part in social and economic life. We need to tackle barriers to participation and change culture so that equal opportunities and equal treatment become a priority for all.
>
> (www.equalities.gov.uk/equality/project/making_it_happen/cons_doc.htm)

The government has actively promoted a more equal society through its policies and through legislative change. The establishment of the Disability Rights Commission (DRC) was a key step. This has since been replaced by the Equality and Human Rights Commission as part of the Equality Act (2006). Similarly, the

Race Relations Amendment Act (2000) signalled a powerful commitment to change by placing a duty to promote race equality and good race relations to over 40,000 public bodies, which includes further education organisations. Policies and programmes across the breadth of government aim to improve outcomes for disadvantaged groups and respond to diverse needs. Examples of these are as follows.

- The New Deal 50 Plus is currently developing new work-based training opportunities designed to help older people retrain, particularly in sectors which have been reluctant to recruit older people.

- The Jobcentre Plus initiative offers a range of programmes aimed at helping disabled people obtain and keep paid work with specialist support from disability advisors.

You may have had learners attend your programmes that have been referred by a project, scheme or agency such as those mentioned.

Example

Rose teaches information and communication technology (ICT) to learners who are referred through the Lone Parent Support and Achieve Programme. Each learner has their own particular needs in terms of their existing skills and knowledge, and the scope of their work placement. To meet these needs, Rose negotiates an individual learning programme with each learner which also includes a negotiated start and end date. Programmes are designed to take account of each of the learner's interests and requirements of their work place.

In this example, Rose recognises that different learners will bring different perspectives, ideas, opinions, histories, skills, knowledge and culture, and that a traditional ICT programme where the start/end date and programme content are the same for all may not meet the needs of individual learners in these circumstances. When promoting equality and diversity, Rose has shown that she understands how to make adjustments to the programme requirements to suit the learner. Learners should be invited to discuss any adjustments that may be necessary and be actively involved in making decisions about how they will achieve their learning outcomes.

Equality and diversity are now everyone's responsibility and organisations must accept that they should seek to promote these through an integrative approach. Providing redress for individuals suffering discrimination is important; however, public bodies, such as educational establishments, must proactively eliminate discrimination and harassment, rather than waiting for individuals to make a complaint. Organisations should be proactive in promoting equality of opportunity, and not just avoid discrimination. For this to be successful, it requires the active support of all personnel, i.e. teaching staff, support staff, stakeholders, learners, customers and contractors.

You may find that new legislation has been introduced that will have an impact on your learners. It may be that the demographics of your group are different from previous groups. You will need to consider whether you need to make any adjustments to your programme to ensure your learners' experience is effective, i.e. application, recruitment, initial assessment, induction, teaching methodology, assessment and evaluation.

Activity

You have found out that the learners you are teaching next year are predominantly male as a result of direct marketing to this particular group. You have taught this programme before, mainly to females, and have all your activities and resources prepared. What adjustments would you make in advance to prepare for your group?

You may need to consider adjustments to your planning, for example, scheme of work and session plans, and teaching methods depending on the preferred learning styles of your learners. It may be that you will find that male learners prefer to learn by doing (kinaesthetic) and that your existing programme planning does not reflect this. If the gender make-up of the group is different from the previous time you delivered this programme, then you will need to explore what adjustments can be made. This may also involve reviewing the use of any specialist staff, guest speakers or other agencies involved in your programme. You might need to amend your handouts, presentations and activities to reflect both genders.

Promotion of equality

The fundamental reason for promoting equality is to meet the needs of individual learners. Individuals are at the heart of the education system, and meeting their needs requires an active approach to equality of opportunity at all stages of their learning journey. It is about the removal of social and economic barriers to participation. Good equal opportunities practices ensure that all learners:

- are respected and not discriminated against;
- become aware of equality and inclusion;
- benefit from high-quality opportunities to learn;
- learn in an environment that supports their development.

The Learning and Skills Council (LSC) look to employers and learning organisations they fund to help promote equality of opportunity, widen participation and improve performance. They recommend the following.

Explicit references:

- equality of opportunity should be promoted and discrimination tackled so that all learners achieve their potential;

- guidance and support should be sensitive to equality of opportunity;

- organisations should have effective measures to eliminate oppressive behaviour, including all forms of harassment;

- programmes should be socially inclusive, ensuring equality of access and opportunities for learners;

- teachers should use materials and teaching methods that promote equality of opportunity;

- there should be explicit aims, values and strategies promoting equality for all that are reflected in the organisation's work.

Implicit references:

- learners should have access to relevant, effective support on personal issues;

- learners should understand their rights and responsibilities;

- learning resources and accommodation should allow all learners to participate fully;

- organisations should promote good working relationships that foster learning;

- programmes should be responsive to local circumstances;

- the organisation's values should be fully understood by staff, including subcontractors and work-placement organisations;

- the performance of different groups of learners should be used to guide programme development.

You need to take positive steps to promote a culture of equality and diversity in everything you do, that may affect the learning experience. The following are some practical suggestions you could use.

Marketing and recruitment

- Actively market under-represented groups as identified by government policies.

- Ensure all promotional materials are inclusive and do not stereotype.

- Ensure application forms gather equal opportunities data, also known as impact data.

- Ensure your equal opportunities policy is explicit in any marketing and recruitment materials and practice, and in early discussions with your learners.

Induction and initial assessment

- Carry out relevant initial assessment and diagnostic tests.

- Check that your learners and any support staff understand the equality and diversity policies and procedures, act on them and know where they can be accessed.

- Consider how effective teaching and learning are for your learners, following analysis of their initial assessment tests and identification of their learning styles.

- Consider how well your learners are guided and supported.

- Ensure the learning environment is welcoming to all, irrespective of age, disability, gender, race, religion and belief, and sexual orientation.

- Find out from your learners if they require any adjustments to be made to the environment, equipment or resources. If so, ensure this is carried out.

- Identify and remove barriers, within your control, which hinder or prevent learners from achieving their full potential.

- Inform learners of who they can contact in case of a query or problem.

- Respect confidentiality at all times.

Teaching and learning

- Consider how well your programme and activities meet the needs and interests of all your learners.

- Ensure all teaching and learning materials are inclusive, use clear language and don't contain too much jargon.

- Ensure the environment is free from potential hazards, for example, moving bags and coats out of the way.

- Make arrangements to meet cultural, religious or faith needs.

- Prepare well in advance to make adjustments to programme requirements and session plans.

- Provide adapted materials where needed.

- Seek opportunities within your programme delivery to celebrate cultural diversity, widen your learners' cultural understanding and prepare them to be effective citizens in a diverse society.

- Take positive action to provide individual encouragement and support to all learners.

- Talk to learners for whom adjustments have been made, to ensure these are successful.

- Utilise support services within the organisation.

Assessment

- Ensure that your assessment methods follow the rules of VACSR (valid, authentic, current, sufficient and reliable).

- Find out what the Awarding/Examining body's policy is with regard to access to assessment.

- Know what adjustments to make to assessments and examinations to enable all your learners to have the opportunity to achieve their potential.

- Liaise with others as necessary.

Evaluation

- Consult with learners who have received additional support to obtain feedback regarding their experience, and use the outcomes to guide further action.

- Evaluate your sessions to ensure you are implementing equality and diversity policies effectively, and are embracing inclusivity.

- Obtain feedback from your learners to show that adjustments have been implemented.

Try to be proactive and meet your learners' needs as soon as you become aware of them.

Example

Kevin has declared to you during his initial programme interview that he is transgender and wants to know which toilet facilities he can use. He has not asked that this information remain confidential.

This declaration by your learner means that your whole organisation is deemed to know under the Disability Discrimination Act (DDA) Part Four (1995 amended 2005) and will need to make reasonable adjustments so that Kevin has access to toilet facilities he is comfortable with. It might be suggested by your organisation that Kevin can use the disabled toilet which is accessed by both males and females. If your organisation is unable to respond to Kevin's needs, he may feel that under the Gender Reassignment Regulations (1999) his needs have not been given the same consideration as those of male and female gender.

Some learners may not want to complete the section on their application form which requires them to disclose details such as a disability, ethnic origin, date of birth, etc. It might not be compulsory; however, the information will help your organisation support learners, as well as collect data for purposes such as funding, and statistics to inform policies.

Tackling inequality is about social justice and the rationale for dealing with it is based on developing a fairer society. This argument is based on the belief that everyone should have a right to equal access to employment. When employed, they should have equal pay and equal access to training and development, as well as being free of any direct or indirect discrimination and harassment or bullying. This can be described as the right to be treated fairly, and your organisation should aim to:

- develop equality of opportunity, i.e. ensure that learners have the freedom to follow their own learning style, and have the chance to take an appropriate programme;

- develop equality of outcome, i.e. ensure that learners have an equal chance of achievement;

- develop equality of process, i.e. treat learners in the same way through teaching and learning;

- widen participation opportunities to reach all areas of the local community and society.

It is important that your organisation has a consistent approach to tackling victimisation and discrimination. This will make it easier for teachers and learners to identify and change unfair practices. It is your responsibility to manage the learning experience and deal with any inequalities that occur. Dr Morris Massey (2008), an American psychologist, carried out research on how values are formed and what they mean. He stated that by the time we reach 21 our value system is more or less fixed. However, it can be changed if you experience a significant emotional event, for example, birth, death, divorce, etc. However, it does not have to be a dramatic event, but something that really strikes a chord, for example, a learning experience. You may have heard your learners describe their learning as *something that has changed their lives*. This demonstrates the impact that a positive learning experience has on your learners, and conversely a bad learning experience through some form of inequality or discrimination. Good teachers are also described by learners as having a huge impact on their behaviour and attitudes as a result of a learning experience. These teachers are positive role models, having reached their learners on an individual basis. The most affected learners might not have engaged with education in their past; perhaps they had a bad learning experience, or a poor teacher.

You should be proactive in thinking about what you need to do to ensure equality in your classroom practice, before the start of your programme. Make sure you consider: planning, delivery, equality and diversity, and resources.

- Planning: is there anything in the learning environment and surrounding areas that make it inaccessible for any learners?

- Delivery: have you included in your scheme of work and session plans opportunities for differentiated activities?

- Equality and diversity: do you make reference to and use examples from a variety of cultures, religions, traditions, exploring stereotyping and other topics around equality?

- Resources: are people from diverse backgrounds, socio-economic, cultural, and people with disabilities visible in programme materials?

Addressing inequality throughout your teaching will help deal with any issues as they arise. The following are some strategies you could use with your learners:

- learn names and use them regularly;

- negotiate and set appropriate ground rules;

- use an appropriate icebreaker;

- allocate time during induction for information and discussion on equality and diversity, including policies, for example, complaints;

- schedule discussions with learners who require additional support at the beginning and throughout the programme;

- ask your learners about their experience with your organisation at strategic points throughout the programme, i.e. after induction, midway and at the end.

Activity

Evaluate a programme you have taught with a focus on equality and diversity. Check your scheme of work, session plans and resources and draw up an equality and diversity improvement plan to implement the next time you teach this programme.

By carrying out an evaluation of your actions, you should be able to analyse whether these improvements have had a positive impact on your programme's retention and achievement rates, and gain positive feedback from questionnaires. This data will be collated by your organisation and used by funding bodies such as the LSC and Ofsted to measure the overall effectiveness of your learners' journey.

There may still be occasions where behaviours exist that are offensive or distressing. This behaviour may be obvious, but it can also be unintentional and subtle. It may involve nicknames, teasing, name-calling or excluding someone, which is not with malicious intent but which is upsetting. If this should happen in your group of learners it is your organisation's responsibility, through you, to tackle any inappropriate comments or behaviour. All organisations need to examine existing arrangements to ensure they promote fairness and equality. Macpherson (1999, 28) defines discrimination as:

> *The collective failure of an organisation to provide an appropriate and professional service to people because of their colour, culture or ethnic origin. It can be seen or detected in processes, attitudes and behaviour which amount to discrimination through unwitting prejudice, ignorance, thoughtlessness and racist stereotyping which disadvantage minority ethnic people.*

You need to know what steps your organisation requires you to take to prevent discrimination, and take this action when inappropriate behaviour occurs. There are various ways of managing this, depending on the circumstances.

- Build on learner diversity within the group.

- Challenge prejudice and stereotyping as it happens.

- Encourage your learners to confidentially discuss any behaviour during the programme that may give them cause for concern.

- Ensure all resources are inclusive.

- Establish what is acceptable behaviour at the start of the programme.

- If any learners leave, find out why.

- Plan the integration of equality and diversity in your programme delivery.

Example

Jerome has attended a week's summer school programme as part of his Post-Graduate Certificate in Education (PGCE). All learners were required to give the teacher their name, telephone number and relationship of an emergency contact. The completed forms were left on the teacher's desk where they could be seen by other learners. As a result it becomes common knowledge amongst the group that Jerome has a same-sex partner. Jerome is distressed and leaves the programme.

You are required to treat personal information in the strictest confidence and your learners will trust you with details about their private lives. Information about learners should not become common knowledge via their teacher. The impact on this learner is that he was unable to achieve his qualification. This situation constitutes harassment and/or a breach of the Data Protection Act (1998).

Benefits of diversity

Diversity may be considered in terms of demographics (gender, age, ethnicity) but also in terms of skills, background, experience, attitude, personality, work, experience and understanding. It is about visible and non-visible differences. While equality is about treating everyone equally in terms of rights, status and opportunities, with an emphasis on eradicating discrimination, diversity is about making sure that everyone is valued and included.

The Chartered Institute of Personnel and Development states:

> *Diversity is ... the concept that people should be valued as individuals for reasons related to business interests, as well as for moral and social reasons. It recognises that people from different backgrounds can bring fresh ideas and perceptions which can make the way work is done more efficient, and products and services better.*
> (www.cipd.co.uk/subjects/dvsequl/general/divover.htm)

Having a diverse group of staff puts an organisation in a stronger position to meet the needs of their diverse learners, offer a richer and more effective learning experience, and provide role models. However, many organisations continue to take a compliance-only approach to the issue of diversity from the top down, thus missing out on benefits, such as improved creativity, innovation and customer service that arise from a more wholehearted approach to diversity. Successful organisations will recognise the need for immediate action and are ready and willing to spend resources on managing diversity.

Your learners will benefit from:

- a greater understanding of the diverse groups of potential and existing learners represented, meeting their needs more effectively;

- a greater variety of solutions to problems;

- better communication with diverse groups of potential and existing learners;

- greater access to a wider range of individual strengths, experiences, talents and ideas through a diverse collection of skills and perspectives;

- varying points of view providing a larger pool of ideas and experiences.

Diversity in further and adult education should include all types of learners engaging in a wide number of subject specialist areas and disciplines. The benefit of this will lead to a greater number of people from different backgrounds being able to seek an education. *Andragogy*, initially defined as *the art and science of helping adults learn* (Knowles, 1978), currently defines an alternative to pedagogy (teacher-centred learning) and refers to learner-focused education for people of all ages. In other words, an andragogical approach is all about giving the learner control. In the past, learners were shunned who could not fit into the pedagogical formal learning system, as being difficult. As a result many people ended up wasting their lives without achieving an education, because they were not taught according to their learning styles or perceptive skills. For example, people with autism have been found to focus on the tiny details of information rather than the bigger picture, as the average person might.

Learners are now more involved with negotiating and directing their learning. Teachers adapt their teaching methods to take account of the needs of all their learners, ensuring the learning environment fits with the learners and not the other way round. The benefit here is that more learners engage in educational activities and stay with their learning until they have achieved their aim.

A diverse group of learners can be a valuable educational resource that enhances the learning experience. You should try to get a sense of how your learners feel about the cultural climate in your group and encourage your learners to explore perspectives outside of their own experiences. Providing opportunities for all your learners to get to know each other will enable them to recognise diverse backgrounds and special interests. In group discussions, scenarios, case studies and feedback from activities, your learners will have the opportunity to listen and become more informed about cultures other than their own.

Embracing diversity encourages your learners to overcome their stereotypes and biases as they relate to age, disability, gender, race, religion and belief, and sexual orientation.

Activity

Reflect on the systems and structures within your organisation which promote diversity, and identify those which you think are working and those which are not. What can you do to make improvements? What do you think the challenges would be for your organisation?

Taking full advantage of the benefits of diversity is not without its challenges.

- Communication: perceptual, cultural and language barriers need to be overcome for diversity to succeed. Try to foster an attitude of openness by encouraging all learners to express their ideas and opinions and attribute an equal sense of value to all.

- Resistance to change: there are always some learners and staff who will refuse to accept the fact that the social and cultural make-up of society is changing. The notion of *we've always done it this way* inhibits new ideas and progress. This can be counteracted by involving all learners and staff in creating and implementing diversity initiatives in your learning environment.

Diversity not only involves how people perceive themselves but how they perceive others, and those perceptions affect their interactions. There can still be diversity even when there is not a significant minority group, as all individuals are different.

Summary

In this chapter you have learnt about:

- applying and promoting the principles of equality and diversity;

- promotion of equality;

- benefits of diversity.

References and further information

Clements, P and Spinks, T (2000) *The equal opportunities handbook.* London: Kogan Page

Leitch, Lord S (2006) *The Leitch review of skills. Prosperity for all in the global economy: world class skills.* Final Report. London: HMSO

Learning and Skills Council (2007) *Single equality scheme: our strategy for equality and diversity.* London: Learning and Skills Council

Macpherson, Sir W (1999) *The Macpherson report.* London: The Stationery Office

Massey, M, in IODA (2008) *Diversity, fairness and equality information booklet.* IODA

Websites

Chartered Institute for Personnel and Development – www.cipd.co.uk/subjects/dvsequl/general/divover.htm

Equality and diversity: making it happen – www.equalities.gov.uk/equality/project/making_it_happen/cons_doc.htm

Equality and Human Rights Commission – www.equalityhumanrights.com

Knowles: Andragogy and pedagogy – www.infed.org/thinkers/et-knowl.htm

Introduction

In this chapter you will learn about:

- demonstrating good practice;
- adapting learning situations and resources;
- developing strategies for dealing with discrimination.

There are activities and examples to help you reflect on the above which will assist your understanding of how to demonstrate appropriate behaviour.

The appendices contain useful pro-formas you may wish to use.

This chapter contributes towards the following: scope (S), knowledge (K) and practice (P) aspects of the professional standards (A–F domains) for teachers, tutors and trainers in the Lifelong Learning Sector:

AS3,AS5,AS6,AS7,AK3.1,AP3.1,AK5.2,AP5.2,AK6.1,AP6.1,AK6.2,AP6.2,
AK7.1,AP7.1,AK7.2,AP7.2;
BS1,BS2,BS3,BS4,BS5,BK1.2,BP1.2,BK2.1,BP2.1,BK2.5,BP2.5,BK3.4,
BP3.4, BK4.1, BP4.1, BK5.2, BP5.2;
CS1, CS3, CK1.2, CP1.2, CK3.2, CP3.2;
DS1, DS2, DK1.1, DP1.1, DK1.3, DP1.3, DK2.1, DP2.1, DK2.2, DP2.2;
ES1,ES2,ES3,ES4,EK1.2,EP1.2,EK2.1,EP2.1,EK2.4,EP2.4,EK3.1,EP3.1,
EK3.2, EP3.2, EK4.1, EP4.1;
FS1, FS4, FK1.1, FP1.1, FK1.2, FP1.2, FK4.1, FP4.1, FK4.2, FP4.2;

The standards can be accessed at:
www.lluk.org.uk/documents/professional_standards_for_itts_020107.pdf.

Demonstrating good practice

It is important to recognise that to practise equality and diversity effectively and with maximum impact on your learners, they need to be embedded throughout your organisation. Equality and diversity policies need to be well known and regularly practised by all staff so that your organisation can respond to the diversity, differences and inequalities among your learners, staff and community at large. Policies should underpin a flexible programme that identifies individual and local/community needs, and can be adapted to meet changing needs. The diagram below demonstrates how they fit together.

Achieving equality of opportunity through inclusive learning and widening participation (NIACE, 2002)

Teaching adult learners may bring you face-to-face with many diverse environments, situations and people. You may teach in a further education college, adult community learning centre, work-based learning centre, in a community venue or in the workplace. You could experience learners:

- aged 14 upwards;

- whose first language is not English;

- who have had negative experiences of education in the past;

- who have mobility or learning difficulties.

Your learners should always be placed at the heart of everything you do, and all the procedures and systems put in place by your organisation should support this. This is known as a learner-centred approach. The Tomlinson Report (1996) promoted a learner-centred approach that makes learners' individual needs the starting point of the teaching and learning process. Instead of your learner having to fit in with existing provision being offered by learning providers, Tomlinson makes the case for fitting the provision around the needs of your learner:

> *By inclusive learning we mean the greatest degree of match or fit between how learners learn best, what they need and want to learn, and what is required from the sector, a college and teachers for successful learning to take place.*
>
> (Tomlinson, 1996)

This involves every stage of the training cycle, i.e. identifying learners' specific and additional needs; designing a programme that responds to these needs; providing appropriate methods, resources and support while facilitating learning, giving learners access to fair assessment, and gaining feedback as part of the evaluation process.

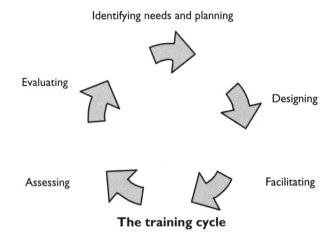

The training cycle

The inclusive approach should help you demonstrate good practice and ensure equality of opportunity for all learners. A quick response to addressing any specific needs is vital to building the confidence of your learners and maintaining their motivation. You should create an understanding of, and communication between, all your learners, to embrace equality and diversity within your organisation.

People are disabled by their environment – the attitudes of others and the policies, practices and procedures of organisations.

(www.diseed.org.uk)

Your learners' experiences of your organisation may have already begun before they arrive for their first session. They may have obtained information perhaps from a brochure or website, or have visited the learning environment and met some of the staff. Equality and diversity policies, practices and procedures need to be embedded across the organisation to enable learners to start their journey with an open and inclusive learning experience from their first welcome to their completion.

Example

An information leaflet in English for prospective learners includes details of crèche provision. Many learners come to the centre whose first language is not English, and do not have other childcare arrangements. This leaflet is therefore not accessible to these learners. Following an analysis of languages spoken in this community, the leaflet has now been produced in two other languages.

Meeting the potential needs of learners will help remove barriers. Other barriers could include transport or financial problems. If funding was available, organisations could help with these, and advertise the details.

Activity

Find out and analyse in your organisation how accessible programme information is to prospective learners. Is information produced or available in different formats to meet potential varying needs of learners? How proactive is your organisation in promoting this?

Before the start of your programme, you need to find out if any of your learners have already shared information about themselves to someone in your organisation. They may have previously completed a programme in another subject. If they have completed an enrolment form they will have been asked if they have a learning difficulty or disability. At this first stage some learners will willingly share this information and some will not. Some learners may not see themselves as having a disability but recognise that they have particular requirements. If a learner has been disadvantaged in the past, they may not tell anyone in these early stages about difficulties they may have. However, if a learner does disclose a disability or additional need to one person, the whole organisation is deemed to know. You need to create an atmosphere whereby your learners feel they can talk to you in confidence if they want to tell you about any particular needs, or if they have needs they feel are not being addressed. Your learner might tell you that they don't want anyone else to know about their learning difficulty or disability. This makes it difficult for you to put in place appropriate reasonable adjustments for that learner, and you would tactfully need to discuss this with them to reach an appropriate outcome.

Learners will feel much more confident about disclosure from the beginning if they feel that the organisation as a whole has a positive and supportive attitude towards anyone who has additional needs. All organisations must take reasonable steps to encourage disclosure. It is good practice to:

- talk to your learner to find out how you can help them;
- find out how long any necessary adjustments will take and follow up where necessary;
- keep your learner informed about progress and timescales.

Example

A learner has told you during her interview that she has Asperger's syndrome, and finds it difficult to sit still for long periods of time. She doesn't want the others on the programme to know about this. You ask her how you can help her and discuss various options. You reassure her that there will be plenty of practical activities involving moving around the learning environment during the sessions.

It may be that further into the programme, once your learner gets to know the others she will feel comfortable disclosing this, but for now you have negotiated a reasonable adjustment that she is comfortable with. The impact in this particular example is that the learner will come to the first session less worried than she would have otherwise been, and enjoy an effective learning experience. It is important that this process is documented in the learner's individual learning plan and your own planning documentation. It will provide evidence of the steps you've taken should it be required, and, more importantly, demonstrate any impact on the learner.

Learners will not always disclose, or perhaps even recognise, that they have any particular requirements. Getting to know your learners will help you identify any needs they may have, to be able to support them appropriately. *Learner support* is generic support relating to the learning experience, for example, advice, counselling, crèche, study skills, etc. *Learning support* is specific support relating to the achievement of the qualification such as literacy, numeracy and ICT.

Example

Chris knows he has difficulty with spelling, is embarrassed by this, and therefore hasn't informed his teacher. In group work he always offers to give the oral feedback and has become very adept at side-stepping any written tasks.

If producing written evidence is an important activity and is assessed as part of your programme, then you would need to plan this in the various activities from the start. An individual written task about the learner's own experiences as part of their initial assessment would clarify their literacy level early on in the programme to enable appropriate support if necessary.

Inclusive learning is about recognising that each of your learners is different and that this is the starting point for developing and planning their learning programme. You should plan your teaching and learning sessions to enable all of your learners to take part, and at the end of the programme achieve their learning goals. This involves identifying their generic and specific needs, providing appropriate resources and support, meeting their preferred learning styles and encouraging them to try new ones, and giving access to fair assessment.

> *The aim is not for students to simply take part in further education but to be actively included and fully engaged in their learning. At the heart of our thinking lies the idea of match or fit between how the learner learns best, what they need and want to learn and what is required from the FE sector, the college and teachers for successful learning to take place.*
>
> (Tomlinson, 1996)

When planning your teaching, you should:

- identify and organise specialist help and be aware of any learner support needed outside of the teaching environment, for example, refreshment areas, toilets, parking, etc.;

- plan to use a variety of teaching methods taking account of learning preferences;

- create, design and/or select appropriate resources and activities;

- encourage social, cultural and recreational activities relevant to the programme (if applicable);

- ensure that all learners are included in group activities and be aware of how group dynamics can sometimes exclude an individual;

- organise individual arrangements in good time for examinations or assessments, for example, apply to Awarding/Examining bodies for approval where extra time is needed;

- provide opportunities for comments and suggestions.

You should be proactive when planning and providing an inclusive learning environment, rather than reactive, to ensure equality of opportunity in all aspects of the learning experience.

Activity

Consider how you would promote inclusive learning and equality of opportunity throughout your teaching. How would you give support for and due regard to:

- *any specific learning difficulties and/or disabilities;*

- *any generic learner needs;*

- *learners who do not disclose they have a particular requirement;*

- *any occurrences of discrimination or stereotyping;*

- *any language barriers?*

To give support and due regard to learners, you can:

- ensure learners are on the right programme;

- liaise with relevant experts to organise a support worker with expertise in a particular learning disability;

- reflect on and evaluate each session as soon as possible afterwards to consider how you might do things differently;

- revisit resources to check that they embrace equality and diversity;

- discuss with learners whose first language is not English whether their level of skill meets the requirements for your programme.

Organisations should invest in equality and diversity development and training for all staff. This will create a culture of support and commitment by all. Attending staff training and keeping up to date with equality and diversity issues will raise your awareness and confidence to respond to your learners' particular needs, and any discriminatory or challenging behaviour. Staff development, training, and information might be incorporated into:

- curriculum and team meetings;
- external verification;
- induction;
- internal verification and standardisation meetings;
- mentoring;
- peer support and/or observations;
- programme/curriculum reviews;
- staff briefing/one-day training sessions/conferences;
- the intranet, information leaflets and staff handbook.

As a teacher you are required to attend training opportunities to keep up to date with amendments, additions to legislation and practice, and changes to Awarding/Examining body procedures, as well as to record this on your CPD record. Your professional registration with the Institute for Learning (IfL) requires you to complete 30 hours of CPD pro-rata on the number of hours you teach per year.

Example

At Ibrahim's recent appraisal, he felt he needed training regarding diversity in the learning environment. He will therefore attend a session to update his knowledge, and will put into practice what he learns.

CPD will help you improve your own attitudes and behaviour, to ultimately improve your learners' experience. You will also have the opportunity to reflect on how this will impact on your professional role as a teacher. Participation in CPD activities provides a good forum for you to use your reflective thinking. There is a checklist for promoting equality and diversity in Appendix 4 which will help develop your practice.

Adapting learning situations and resources

Being different can mean being disadvantaged or discriminated against. Promoting equality and diversity is therefore the key to giving a positive learning experience. The fact that one of your learners may be different in some way is often based upon qualities or characteristics that cannot be changed. You therefore need to reduce barriers, change attitudes and behaviour, and include all learners throughout your sessions.

You may need to adapt various situations as they arise – for example, if a discussion becomes biased, create an opportunity to discuss both sides of the argument. You might also have to adapt resources, for example, to ensure minority groups are represented.

You are in a good position to influence equality of opportunity by providing a learning environment that positively involves all your learners, and is free from favouritism and discrimination, where your learners are treated with respect.

The Disability Discrimination Act (DDA) Part Four (1995 amended 2005) presents a challenge to all teachers. It requires you to anticipate the needs of learners with a disability and that reasonable adjustments are in place to make sure that they are not placed at a disadvantage. This will ensure suitable provision is anticipated and available, rather than the learner having to adapt to the provision that is offered. Organisations and all their staff need to focus on the needs of individual learners and be ready to be flexible in the way that they are organised and their pro-grammes are structured. Some ways in which reasonable adjustments could be sensibly anticipated to meet the needs of learners include the following.

Equipment and environment	This should take account of the needs of diverse users. For example, an adjustable-height workstation would ensure access for any learner who uses a wheelchair. Specialist ICT software or hardware could be used. Ramps could be used to ensure access. Refreshment and toilet areas should be accessible.
Feedback and evaluations	This should be obtained from all learners to ensure current practices are responsive to their needs, and help anticipate future learners' requirements. Not all learners are able to provide feedback in hard copy, therefore electronic questionnaires, e-mail or mobile technology might be more appropriate.
Information	This should be accessible to all. Electronic mail (e-mail) might be an appropriate alternative to noticeboards or leaflets. Signs and notices could be in different languages.
Liaising with others	The responsibility for all adjustments which may be required should be shared. Where organisations such as the Careers Service work with learners, learners would have to agree for their disclosure to be shared with them, since the DDA Act gives providers the duty to comply with learners' requests for confidentiality. Language interpreters may be required and/or staff who can lip-read or use sign language.

Programme resources	Handouts and presentations could be adapted to other formats to make them accessible to all, for example, large print, use of coloured paper. Consider the appropriateness of the level of the language or jargon used in relation to the subject level. Ensure equipment is working and accessible.
Promotional materials	These should demonstrate the organisation's thoughtfulness about ways in which programme provision can take account of the needs of all learners, including those who declare they have a disability. They should also be available in different formats to reach all potential learners.
Staff development	This should ensure staff are well informed of current policies, and the types of needs of learners, in time for that knowledge to be meaningful and have an impact.

When you are planning and devising your programme, it is important to think about what it is that you expect learners to be able to do in order for them to be successful in their learning, and to consider the question: *what if (for whatever reason) they can't do that?* You may want to think about anticipating the likelihood that you will not be able to predict all reasonable adjustments.

Example

David attends a local community centre where he is enrolled on a confidence building programme. The classroom is upstairs and David can only access this via the lift. On the morning of his third session he received a telephone call from the teacher to tell him that the lift was broken and the class had been moved to another room on the ground floor so that he could still attend. David was informed that all other learners on the programme had also been contacted.

In this case the organisation and the teacher were proactive in making alternative arrangements and informed David before he arrived at the centre. This avoided an embarrassing situation for David and the other learners in the very public reception area. Always try to anticipate the needs of your learners, and adapt any situations or resources as required.

Developing strategies for dealing with discrimination

Discrimination often occurs in the learning environment. Discrimination is about treating a person or group differently, often in a negative manner, usually as a result of prejudice. It is about people being thought of as having different worth or value, or given fewer opportunities. However, not all differential treatment is discriminatory. Discrimination occurs when differential treatment cannot be objectively and reasonably justified.

The Human Rights Act (1998) prohibits discrimination on a wide range of grounds including sex, race, colour, language, religion, political or other opinion, national or social origin, association with a national minority, property, birth or other status.

The case law relating to this right has shown that the term *other status* includes, among other things, sexual orientation, illegitimacy, marital status, trade union membership, transsexualism and imprisonment. It can also be used to challenge discrimination on the basis of age or disability.

Example

A prospective learner made some enquiries about learning French at her local learning centre. She obtained some information and advice about the programme at the centre office from one of their staff. As part of this procedure she was asked if she had resided in the country for more than three years, for the purposes of funding. The learner asked if everyone who made enquiries about programmes were asked this same question or if it was only asked of certain groups or learners.

Sometimes discriminatory assumptions are made about people as in this example, i.e. that some learners, because of the amount of time they have resided in the UK, may not be eligible for public funding for their learning. Frontline staff should not make assumptions from the way a person looks or speaks, about whether or not they are eligible for public funding. In other cases, discrimination arises because people have decided that some people deserve to be treated less well than others.

There are two types of discrimination.

- Direct discrimination: where a person is less favourably treated because of their race, sex, marital status, religion, sexual orientation or gender reassignment. This tends to be obvious discrimination; for example, one of your learners requests an extension for a piece of written work, and tells you that the reason is that she is affected by medication for schizophrenia. You don't consider this a valid reason for an extension and decline the request. This is likely to be direct discrimination. You cannot argue that it was not your intention to discriminate; the law only considers the end effect.

- Indirect discrimination: this occurs where a rule, requirement or condition that appears to be fair – because they apply equally to everyone – can be shown to put people from a particular age group or of a particular age at a much greater disadvantage than others, and the rules cannot be objectively justified. An example would be where an organisational policy or practice creates a substantial disadvantage for a disabled person. There is a requirement to adjust the policy for the individual and anticipate the needs of disabled people in general.

In some instances, discrimination may also be positive, i.e. designed to redress perceived injustice. Positive discrimination occurs when a disadvantaged group is treated more favourably in order to overcome an existing situation of inequality. Where it can be objectively and reasonably justified, more favourable treatment in relation to the enjoyment of human rights is permissible under the Human Rights Act (1998).

Example

An organisation has decided not to charge any fees for childcare for adult learners who reside in identified disadvantaged communities. This targets learners who by nature of where they live are already in a situation of inequality. This therefore promotes equality of opportunity by reaching out to groups of people with low skills, who are not currently involved in learning and with a background of low income or disadvantage.

If at any time your learners feel that discrimination has taken place then some sensible steps to adopt include:

● clarify the problem;

● complain within the organisation;

● complain to an external person or organisation;

● get help and advice;

● take legal action;

● try to resolve the issue informally.

Learners should be able to pursue the above process without fear of recrimination. If any form of discrimination or harassment takes place it is stressful and intimidating for the victim. Bullying is also a form of harassment. Examples of this include:

● display or circulation of offensive materials or books;

● ignoring someone;

● intrusive questioning about ethnic origin;

● racist and/or sexist comments or jokes;

● unfair allocation of work;

● unnecessary references to sex;

● unwanted physical contact;

● verbal abuse or taunting.

Activity

Find out all you can about discrimination and harassment. Use the internet and other sources of information. In your experience so far can you think of any instances when you have witnessed any situations in which discrimination or harassment have taken place? What happened and how was it resolved?

When considering forms of harassment, it is important to bear in mind that different people have different cultural and social perceptions as to what they consider to be hostile or degrading. If possible, deliver a workshop session with your learners to try to address these perceptions or assumptions.

During an organisation's recruitment and selection process, teachers are often asked what they understand by equality and diversity and as they ensure it in their teaching. Very often the response is that they would treat everyone the same. However, diversity, fairness and equality are about treating others as they would wish to be treated, rather than making assumptions on their behalf. Your learners are all different and therefore have different needs and different degrees of need which will lead to equal outcomes at the end of their programme.

Language has a fundamental role to play in treating people fairly. Words you use should give a clear message to all your learners that you and your organisation value diversity and respect individual differences. Carefully examining the language you use and the way you use it will help ensure that you treat your learners as individuals and not merely as members of a group. Communication is not just about words, however, and you should also ensure that your tone of voice, demeanour and body language convey the same message of inclusiveness.

Example

Gemma has been asked to plan, design and deliver a four week Job Skills programme as part of a Support and Achieve Programme for Lone Parents. The clients are referred to the programme from JobCentrePlus and the aim of the project is for lone parents to return to work. The very title of this project typecasts these learners into a particular group. They are immediately identified as lone or single parents. Gemma therefore suggests the title be changed.

Reports from the media project an image of lone parents as predominantly young mothers or fathers with children living on their own and claiming state benefits. There are many diverse people who find themselves as lone parents due to different circumstances, for example, widows, widowers or divorcees. The title of a programme can therefore affect who will apply for it; in this example it is positive discrimination in favour of lone parents. However, the content will be based around returning to work and could easily be adapted to suit others, and the mix of learners will help promote inclusion and equality.

Activity

Consider the content of a programme you plan to teach, and think about the language you will use in your documents and resources, for example, session plans, individual learning plans, progress records, teaching materials and resources. Do you think you would use any language which may stereotype or discriminate, or suggest you may prejudge people or groups in negative terms? Have you made up your mind about the group of learners before you even meet them? Can you think of any other groups who may also be subject to this same stereotyping due to the nature of the programme they will be taking?

Examples of other groups of learners who may be subjected to stereotyping are:

- disaffected young people;
- long-term unemployed;
- offenders (ex or current);
- older people;
- people with mental health problems.

When providing a learner-centred approach that makes the specific learning needs of all learners the starting point, organisations need to be flexible in their approach to services being offered to their learners. They also need to know what the sources are that are driving equality and diversity. For example:

- legislation, which is regularly updated or amended;
- significant change in the ethnic make-up of the population, resulting in the need for a greater awareness of differing needs;
- greater expectations of services delivered by organisations, particularly in the public sector;
- significant events followed by reports and recommendations that raise public awareness and highlight the need for change.

Example

Jayne teaches at an adult community learning centre and has a learner who has asked for a private place to pray at a specific time during the programme. With the learner's permission, Jayne approached the centre manager and booked a room for the same time each week so that the learner had some privacy for prayer at the time requested. Jayne discussed with the learner options for catching up with the work missed while he was away from the programme delivery.

To address inclusion, organisations need to know about situations and how they impact on the services they provide. All staff should be kept up to date through CPD.

On this occasion Jayne was able to negotiate with the centre manager for a private room for her learner. Fortunately at this time a room was available – this may not always be the case. However, the organisation must make a reasonable adjustment; but it may not always be possible to respond to every need.

The following are some ways in which you can overcome prejudice and discrimination.

- Being compassionate and sympathetic to various demands of different races and cultures, even when this might cause a negative impact within the group.
- Being genuine in your desire to be fair, and remaining professional at all times.
- Being sensitive and respectful to the thoughts, feelings and opinions of others.
- Demonstrating your knowledge and commitment to equality and diversity, to create a positive atmosphere of trust and respect.
- Raising awareness within the group of the differences between people, and being aware of the impact of behaviour upon others.
- Setting ground rules and using an appropriate icebreaker.
- Showing empathy by putting yourself in the other person's position and imagining how they might think and feel in the circumstances, then looking back at your own behaviour from their perspective.
- Thinking through the consequences of actions that may stop you or your learners making a prejudicial comment that might offend someone.
- Valuing the experiences of others, and incorporating this into your sessions.

Think of equality and diversity as being an extension of the skills and knowledge that you already have and use, during your teaching and learning sessions with your groups and individuals. Planning ahead will help reduce any potential occurrences of discrimination, and dealing with situations as they arise will help change attitudes.

Summary

In this chapter you have learnt about:

- demonstrating good practice;
- adapting learning situations and resources;
- developing strategies for dealing with discrimination.

References and further information

Clements, P and Spinks, T (2000) *The equal opportunities handbook: how to deal with everyday issues of unfairness.* London: Kogan Page

DfES (2003) *New rights to learn: a tutor guide to teaching adults after the Disability Discrimination Act Part Four*. London: DfES

Hull Adult Education Service (2005) *Disability equality and inclusion*.

Individual Organisation, Development, Assessment (2007) *Diversity, fairness and equality*. IODA

Learning and Skills Council (2005) *Equality and diversity – what's that then?* East Midlands: LSC

Learning and Skills Council (2007) *Single equality scheme: our strategy for equality and diversity*. East Midlands: LSC

Reisenberger, A and Dadzie, S (2002) *Equality and diversity in adult and community learning: a guide for managers*. London: NIACE LSDA

Tomlinson, J (1996) *Inclusive learning*. Further Education Funding Council/HMSO

TUC (2005) *Diversity in diction - equality in action*. Unison

Websites

Disability Discrimination Act – www.opsi.gov.uk

Disability Equality in Education – www.diseed.org.uk

Institute for Learning – www.ifl.ac.uk

University of Strathclyde: Anticipating Reasonable Adjustments, www.strath.ac.uk/disabilityservice/legislation/anticipatingreasonableadjustments/

4 HELPING AND SUPPORTING OTHERS

Introduction

> In this chapter you will learn about:
>
> - identifying inequality;
> - identifying barriers to inclusion;
> - supporting equality and diversity.

There are activities and examples to help you reflect on the above which will assist your understanding of how to help and support others.

The appendices contain useful pro-formas you may wish to use.

This chapter contributes towards the following: scope (S), knowledge (K) and practice (P) aspects of the professional standards (A–F domains) for teachers, tutors and trainers in the Lifelong Learning Sector:

AS1, AS2, AS3, AS4, AS5, AS6, AS7;
AK1.1, AK2.1, AK2.2, AK3.1, AK4.2, AK4.3, AK5.1, AK5.2, AK6.1, AK6.2, AK7.1;
AP1.1, AP2.1, AP2.2, AP3.1, AP5.1, AP5.2, AP6.1, AP6.2, AP7.1;
BS1, BS2, BS3, BS4, BS5;
BK1.1, BK1.2, BK1.3, BK2.1, BK2.2, BK2.3, BK2.5, BK3.1, BK3.2, BK3.3, BK3.4, BK4.1, BK5.1, BK5.2;
BP1.1, BP1.2, BP1.3, BP2.1, BP2.2, BP2.3, BP2.4, BP2.5, BP3.4, BP3.5, BP4.1, BP5.1, BP5.2;
CS2, CS4;
CK1.2, CK2.1, CK3.2, CK3.3, CK3.4, CK3.5;
CP1.2, CP2.1, CP3.2, CP3.3, CP3.4, CP3.5, CP4.2;
DS1;
DK1.1; DK2.1, DK2.2;
DP1.1, DP1.3; DP2.1, DP2.2;
ES2, ES3;
EK2.1, EK3.1; EK3.2;

EP2.1, EP3.1, EP3.2;
FS1, FS2, FS4;
FK1.1, FK1.2, FK2.1, FK4.1, FK4.2;
FP1.1, FP1.2, FP2.1, FP4.1; FP4.2.

The standards can be accessed at:
www.lluk.org.uk/documents/professional_standards_for_itts_020107.pdf.

Identifying inequality

When teaching, you will want to be fair and treat all your learners equally, but may be concerned that you or another learner will say or do something that will offend or upset someone. You will need to identify forms of inequality in your teaching and in your organisation, to alleviate any negative impact this might have. Forms of inequality are broader than those covered by the six strands of equality, and can be divided into two dimensions.

Primary: things which are inherent or quite visible	**Secondary:** things which are less obvious or less visible
Age	Ability and intelligence/skills
Attitude	Criminal background
Colour	Disability – mental
Culture	Education
Disability – physical	Family background and status
Dress	Financial status
Ethnicity	Health
Gender	Home environment
Language, accent, dialect	Race
Physical appearance	Religion or belief
Sexuality	Social position

The table lists areas against which many people show prejudice and therefore may be the target for discriminatory practices. As a teacher you will need to be aware of the legislation that will impact on you and your organisation's relationship with your learners. You will also need to be aware of how you relate to the above dimensions, particularly those in the secondary category, which are less obvious or less visible. Sometimes prejudices can be innate and you need to reflect on your own attitudes, values and beliefs and subsequent behaviours, and whether or not your learners are affected by this.

Example

Bernie is the arts and design curriculum manager for an adult community learning service. He has been asked to organise a creative arts programme for a group of young people who are not in employment, education or training (NEET). He asks for a volunteer from his team. No one comes forward. Bernie talks to some of the teachers about this and they say they don't want to teach in disadvantaged areas with young people who have issues or problems.

This example shows how some dimensions, such as age, criminal records, education, family background and home environment, can relate to preconceived ideas about certain groups, which are probably wrong. In the advert, these young people were identified as NEET, leading Bernie's staff to make certain assumptions. This form of inequality results in difficulties in recruiting teachers to work with these particular groups, which can exacerbate feelings of social exclusion among young people who are NEET.

Activity

Can you think of a time when you have turned down an offer of teaching because you have had preconceived ideas about what the learners would be like?

Everyone has conscious and unconscious preferences which influence their thoughts (prejudice) and actions (discrimination). It is the unconscious prejudices that can lead people to make pre-judgements based on little or no fact, regardless of what is consciously known to be true. The relationship between prejudice and discrimination will have an impact on your learners. There are four main relationships between prejudice and discrimination. The table gives examples.

You can be prejudiced and discriminatory	You believe that young people in general display offensive behaviour and don't want to learn. You don't teach classes where learners are young people.
You can be non-prejudiced yet still discriminate	You believe that there is some good in everyone and that all young people deserve opportunities. Your curriculum manager tells you that young people are difficult to work with and it is best to avoid any teaching which involves this group. You do this because you don't want to contradict him.
You can be prejudiced yet not discriminate	You tell your curriculum manager that you believe he is being discriminatory and he

	retracts his advice to you. However, he has not changed his mind about young people, he has simply altered his behaviour.
You can be both non-prejudiced and non-discriminatory	You are now both non-prejudiced and non-discriminatory due to your knowledge and experience.

The next activity is the *implicit association test*. You will find the experience interesting and informative and it will give you an insight into the ways in which your unconscious prejudices impact on your behaviour and ultimately the way in which you communicate with your learners.

Activity

Access the website below and try to describe your self-understanding of one of the topics listed. Then test your conscious versus unconscious preferences ranging from pets to political issues, ethnic groups to sports teams, and entertainers to styles of music. If you are unprepared to encounter interpretations that you might find objectionable, please do not carry out this activity.

https://implicit.harvard.edu/implicit/research/

The results of this activity may tell you something that you are already aware of about yourself or they may give you something to reflect on. The important point is to recognise that judgements are not neutral and that everyone works from a value base. No one exists in a vacuum. This is also an activity you could ask your learners to complete, probably on their own away from the group environment. If all your learners are happy to share their findings, it could lead to a useful discussion.

Every person is a unique individual, but each develops in a social setting in which they are influenced by, and interact with, other people. Every society is located in a particular physical setting. The attitudes and values people have in regard to their environment greatly affect interactions between the person, society, culture and the environment, which will have an impact on their capacity to learn. Environments present societies with both opportunities and restraints. One of the government's priorities for post-16 learning is to increase participation in areas of high deprivation. If you are required to teach in community settings in this environment then you will need to be aware of the forms of inequality and discrimination that some of your learners may have experienced or are currently experiencing. If the individual or group you are teaching know that people have made negative assumptions or have preconceived ideas about them, they will expect to be treated in a particular way because they are perceived to be different. This can make teaching them difficult. The impact on your learners may be a lack of self-confidence and self-esteem, demotivation, unwillingness to try new things and/or poor social skills.

Example

A group of ten young unemployed single mums from a disadvantaged area identified an interest to work in an office. The training manager at the children's centre they attended has asked your organisation to provide a one-week communication skills programme on their premises. At the first session the learners expected to be treated as they did when they were at school and behaved as if they were; for example, throwing things at each other and talking over you.

At school, some of these learners behaved in this way for various reasons and expected it to be the same at their first learning experience as adults. They were perhaps nervous and defensive about the whole experience, which caused them to act the way they did.

Activity

Looking at the above example, what would you have done to manage these disruptions and make the learning experience effective for these learners?

You might have thought about using a suitable icebreaker to help the learners get to know each other better, and then follow this by agreeing some ground rules. This would help establish a starting point, for learning to then take place more effectively. You would need to treat each person as an individual, encouraging their learning and development, and helping them realise they do not have to be classed as single mothers, but people in their own right.

Identifying barriers to inclusion

Inclusion recognises every individual's right to be treated equally, and to be accorded the same access to services and opportunities as everyone else. It is the state of being included. Many people face particular barriers in taking up the opportunities society has to offer; these are known as barriers to inclusion. Often these are associated with particular groups, such as families or pensioners, who are more vulnerable to poverty, or those who are subject to discrimination or disadvantage for reasons of gender, race or disability. Other barriers are more personal and can be directly damaging to an individual's prospects of inclusion, for example, poor health, homelessness or drug misuse. Other barriers may be as simple as a lack of affordable local childcare or transport.

The barriers your learners may experience which would make them feel excluded, and that learning opportunities are not within their reach, include:

● access to childcare;

● access to the location and learning environment;

- age: much younger or older than others in the group;
- bullied in the past;
- cultural differences;
- costs too high;
- different or specific learning needs;
- ethnicity/race/religion;
- family problems or commitments;
- fear of embarrassment;
- fear of joining a group;
- financial reasons;
- having to attend on their own;
- inappropriate learning environment;
- inequality, i.e. stereotyped gender roles;
- knowledge and use of technology;
- lack of support at work to be allowed time off;
- language;
- medical reasons;
- physical/emotional difficulties;
- poor childhood experiences of learning;
- preconceived negative feelings/ideas;
- returning to an educational environment after a long break;
- shy and lacking confidence or self-esteem;
- specific needs or requirements;
- transport difficulties;
- type of teaching, for example e-learning might not be appropriate;
- unidentified fears.

The above are very real for your learners where barriers are linked to practical issues, for example, access to childcare, or emotional issues, such as a lack of self-confidence. The image your organisation, and indeed you as a teacher, portrays can have an effect upon whether your learners decide to attend a programme with you or not.

Example

Sheila teaches an embroidery programme. Her learners have mostly been in her class for four terms, developing their skills and knowledge, and working on projects. As they have been together so long, they all know each other and Sheila very well. A new learner joins the group at the start of the next term; she only stays for three weeks and then doesn't return.

Inclusion means to allow people into a group, i.e. excluding nobody. In this example the form of inequality is that of an individual joining a majority group. The new learner perhaps felt uncomfortable joining a well-established group who were familiar with the teacher, the programme, the environment and the norms in the classroom. Most new learners would find this situation difficult, therefore immediately there is a risk factor involved in retaining this learner; they more than likely felt excluded. You may have learners who join your programme later than others. Always make them feel welcome, introduce them to the others to help them belong, and ensure you help them catch up with what they have missed.

Activity

Can you think of a time in your teaching when a learner has not stayed beyond the first few weeks? Did you find out why the learner decided not to return? Was it something that could have been anticipated and successfully dealt with?

If this has happened in the past, try to find out why – you may be able to encourage your learner to come back again, perhaps by talking to them outside of the learning environment by a telephone call.

Your organisation's equality and diversity policy should include promises to your learners, for example, to:

- actively work against a culture of dependency;
- ensure that individuals are valued in their achievements and progression opportunities are recognised;
- place the learner at the centre of the learning process;
- practise a philosophy of equity as opposed to exclusivity;
- provide a curriculum and support that are relevant to each learner;
- provide an inclusive learning environment to ensure that provision can be made for the learning needs of as wide a cross-section of the general population and local community as possible;

- take account of the diverse range of support needed to enable individuals to participate and learn, and utilise any learning aids or adaptations to resources.

At each stage of their journey, talk to your learners and ask them what works best for them, for example, what they find difficult and what has worked for them in the past. Some learning difficulties and disabilities come with labels, for example Asperger's syndrome, and this may lead to you making assumptions about what you think you need to do to support this learner's learning. By talking to your learners, you can find out if there are any areas you can help and support them with: never assume you know what's best for them.

> Learners' needs should be met through equitable and easily understood systems of planning, funding and placement, enabling all learners to achieve their goals and progress to the maximum possible level of independence and activity in their communities and in employment.
>
> (Learning and Skills Council, 2005)

Example

Musnah has declared on her enrolment form that she has dyslexia. Some learners may need to have handouts copied onto coloured paper. This may not be the case with Musnah – you will only find out how to teach her effectively by discussing with her what support she needs.

Try to develop individual strategies for your learners and don't make assumptions about any learning difficulties or disabilities they may declare to you. This could lead to the nature of the difficulty being misunderstood and leading to inappropriate treatment, including bullying and isolation, resulting in depression. Being uncomfortable in approaching and managing learners with learning difficulties or disabilities can be more about your embarrassment than theirs. All your learners will want to take advantage of the same opportunities as other learners, and to feel like an accepted member of the group.

Activity

Imagine you are teaching a programme of card making. You have been advised that a learner who is deaf has enrolled on your programme and will be supported by a sign language interpreter. What will you need to consider in your preparation for teaching this programme?

You would need to think about how you might adjust your own teaching style to suit that of the learner, how you might design and organise individual and group activities to ensure that everyone understands what they are to do, and can take part. You will need to create and present resources so that everyone can use and read them, and whether or not you need any special equipment. You will also need to ensure there is room for the interpreter to sit by the learner, and that the learner can see everything you demonstrate, as well as seeing others in the group in case they lip-read.

When involving others in the learning process, you need to:

- decide who needs to know what and when, to maintain good communications with your colleagues;

- discuss roles and responsibilities with your support workers at the start of your joint working relationship – where other professionals such as sign language interpreters are involved, they will have their own code of conduct and will be able to brief you about this;

- discuss where support workers will position themselves in the room during various activities to ensure that learners can participate fully and safely;

- explain the plan for each session to any learning assistants, sign language interpreters and bilingual interpreters so that they can explain the key points to learners; they may need guidance on this if they are not familiar with your subject;

- make arrangements to have materials translated into the appropriate medium well before the session, to accommodate learners with literacy and language needs, or a visual impairment;

- make sure that all colleagues understand the principles of safe working and do not present any obstacles during the session;

- set out a clear code of conduct for support workers so that they support their learners without interfering with the progress of the session;

- well before the session, show support workers any written or visual materials you will use so that they can brief learners effectively.

You can obtain more information regarding this from the Quality Improvement Agency website: www.qiaresources4adultlearning.net/.

Try to capture all of your intentions on your scheme of work and session plans; these are working documents for all those involved in the learning experience. It is good practice to plan ways in which learners can work together at some points during your sessions, while having their individual needs met at other times.

On a broader scale, there is a need for transformational change in further and adult education. There is already evidence of emerging good practice, for example, regional/local inter-agency collaboration, and of existing good practice. This good practice should be built upon and extended to enable increased choice of high-quality post-16 provision (appropriate to learners' assessed needs) for those learners with learning difficulties and/or disabilities, which is learner-centred and cost-effective in the use of public funds. It should also enable learners to progress to the maximum possible level of independence and activity in their communities and employment.

Example

Janine delivers and assesses the NVQ in Supporting Teaching and Learning Level 2 at her local college. The curriculum team has planned for the Local Safeguarding Children Board (LSCB) to deliver the knowledge outcomes on child protection.

This good practice is an example of inter-agency collaboration and inviting experts who are occupationally competent in a particular field to deliver specialist parts of the programme.

In moving towards meeting the challenges set out in the Leitch Review of Skills (2006), the Learning and Skills Council (LSC) has developed a *Single Equality Scheme* (2007), which is designed to place equality and diversity at the heart of what they do, i.e. through high-quality education they can create a more socially cohesive society. Christopher N Banks CBE, Chairman, LSC (2007) stated:

We want to do more than comply with the present legislation for equal opportunities. We intend to go beyond it to make our policies and practice fully inclusive, eliminating discrimination, promoting equality and embracing diversity in all its aspects. In doing this we look forward to working with the new Commission for Equality and Human Rights to make sure that the learning and skills sector contributes to fulfilling its vision and objectives.

The LSC has incorporated its Race Equality Scheme, Disability Equality Scheme and Gender Equality Scheme and brought them together into a Single Equality Scheme. This means that the LSC will challenge all their providers on outcomes for learners in relation to equality and diversity against the priorities they have set. These priorities are:

- communities that feel they have a reasonable chance of success;
- employers able to compete in a global economy;
- increased recognition of the value of vocational qualifications;
- more adults getting relevant skills;
- more young people succeeding;
- provision that is relevant to the future;
- qualifications that are recognised and valued in the workplace;
- raising participation.

The Single Equality Scheme sets out the LSC's response to their duties and commitment to promoting equality and diversity which then shapes their priorities. This is then translated into targets for their providers, i.e. your organisation if you receive funding, and then yourself, and how they relate to your learners and the programmes you are teaching.

Activity

Consider the priorities set out by the LSC for the purposes of funding. Can you relate these to the programme(s) you teach? Do you think that your programme(s) fit these priorities?

Where funding is streamlined and particularly focused on very specific priorities, your organisation will be considering the curriculum it offers. It may be that certain programmes will no longer be offered if they do not meet with the LSC's priorities. It is important for you to be aware of the priorities and through CPD to keep up to date with new programmes and developments in your specialist area.

Education plays an important role in helping your learners achieve their potential in life. For some, it can give new opportunities and stop them being trapped in a life of disadvantage. It is therefore important that everybody has access to appropriate educational opportunities.

Recognising the contribution of diversity within society requires everyone to respect other individuals, and to treat them fairly and with dignity. Without respect and good relations between groups, your learners may not be able to take an active part in decisions that affect them, and they may be prevented from fulfilling their potential. A lack of respect between learners from different backgrounds can also contribute to social unrest. Learners should have the opportunity to express their views and beliefs freely, while respecting those of other learners.

Supporting equality and diversity

To support equality and diversity, you need to be able to deal with any issues of harassment or bullying occurring within your sessions.

Harassment includes behaviour that is offensive, frightening or in any way distressing. It may be intentional bullying which is obvious or violent, but it can also be unintentional, subtle and dangerous. It may involve nicknames, teasing, name-calling or other behaviour which is not with malicious intent but which is upsetting or hurtful. It may be about the individual's sexual orientation (real or perceived) or it may be about the sexual orientation (real or perceived) of those with whom the individual associates. It may not be targeted at an individual but consist of a general culture which, for example, appears to tolerate the telling of homophobic jokes.

The Employment Equality (Sexual Orientation) Regulations (2003) apply as equally to the harassment of heterosexual people as they do to the harassment of lesbians, gay men and bisexual people. Organisations may be held responsible for the actions of their staff as well as the staff being individually responsible. If harassment takes place in the workplace or at a time and place associated with the workplace, for example, a work-related social gathering, the organisation may be liable, and may be ordered to pay compensation unless it can be shown that it took reasonable steps to prevent harassment. Individuals who harass may also be ordered to pay compensation.

You should take the following reasonable steps to overcome any problems.

- Know about your organisation's policies and procedures for dealing with your learners' complaints. This should have been shared with learners during induction. The policy should explain:
  - a definition of unacceptable behaviour;
  - how learners can report bullying, harassment or any other forms of unacceptable behaviour;
  - how you and the organisation will deal with unacceptable behaviour.
- Treat all complaints seriously, regardless of who brings them, and investigate the complaint thoroughly.
- Deal quickly and firmly with anyone who acts inappropriately.
- Deal with matters informally and internally if possible. The solution may be as simple as pointing out to a learner the effect that their behaviour has on others and asking them to stop.
- Be consistent, open and fair in all decisions.

As you interact with others of different cultures, there is no good substitute for receptiveness to interpersonal feedback, good observation skills, effective questions and some common sense. There is much to be gained by observing how people of the same culture interact with each other. Don't be afraid to ask questions as most people respond very positively to enquiries about their culture. Ask a variety of people to obtain a balanced view. If you have the opportunity, hold a group discussion to help break down any assumptions.

If you can make a genuine effort to find the positive historical, literary and cultural contributions of a society; learning a few polite expressions in another person's language; and showing appreciation for the food and music of another culture, you can have positive effects upon that person.

In everyday conversation, spoken words are only one way to communicate. As little as 7 per cent of a message may be expressed in words. The rest is through facial expression, voice tone, body gestures and overall posture. When the verbal and non-verbal messages don't match up, people pay more attention to the non-verbal message. That's what's meant by the old saying *a picture is worth a thousand words*.

It may be difficult to understand non-verbal messages because different cultures have different expectations about eye contact, physical touch, body gestures, etc. A person's gender, age, position in society and individual preference can complicate communication even more.

Culture greatly influences attitudes about physical contact, whether it's a handshake, hug, or pat on the back. In Asia, female friends often hold hands and men casually embrace one another as they walk along the street. Americans, however, may feel uncomfortable with such public behaviour. In some cultures, affectionately patting an adult's head is strictly taboo, and pointing with fingers or feet is not acceptable.

How close should people stand to each other when they're having a conversation? In areas of the Middle East and South America, people stand very close when talking. European Americans like to have more distance between them, while some African Americans prefer even more space. You can create great discomfort by standing too close to another person. Not being aware of this can even prevent someone from understanding or accepting the ideas you're trying to convey.

To create a positive environment for communication, your non-verbal message must closely match your verbal message. First, recognise your own expectations about non-verbal communication, and then find ways to learn about those of individuals and other cultures. One way to do this is to carefully observe how people and families speak and behave around each other and with people of authority. This can provide clues about the true meaning of their non-verbal interactions.

Non-verbal messages have a powerful impact on what's communicated. When a person is sensitive to these silent messages, they are far more likely to interact with others in a friendly, comfortable manner and to make the spoken message more understandable.

Differences between cultures and people are real and can add richness (and humour) to your learning programme. People everywhere have much in common, such as a need for affiliation and love, participation and contribution. When the exterior is peeled away, there are not so many differences after all. Learners need to know that they will be comfortable and safe, and that the environment is suitable for their needs.

Example

The local training organisation provides a separate common room for Muslim learners, as well as a prayer room for staff and learners. Food to meet the specific cultural and religious dietary requirements of the community is also provided. There are signs or posters in community languages which are openly displayed.

All learning environments should be welcoming by promoting a multicultural, inclusive ethos, regardless of the ethnic profile of their staff, learners or the local community. This is imperative for organisations with a public commitment to inclusive learning and widening participation. More welcoming messages and positive visual images might be needed. Examples of promoting diversity might include positive and diverse images of learners, multi-faith prayer rooms, and catering facilities with a varied menu for a range of dietary requirements. Where possible, the availability of diverse social facilities for learners is vital as a means of developing and spreading good practice. The development of diverse curricula and policies for the learner, and the value of opportunities provided to work with like-minded groups is key to embracing and supporting equality and diversity within the learning environment.

Summary

In this chapter you have learnt about:

- identifying inequality;

- identifying barriers to inclusion;

- supporting equality and diversity.

References and further information

Clements, P and Spinks, T (2000) *The equal opportunities handbook*. London: Kogan Page

IODA (2008) *Diversity, fairness and equality information booklet*. IODA

Leitch, Lord S (2006) *The Leitch review of skills. Prosperity for all in the global economy: world class skills*. Final Report. London: HMSO

Learning and Skills Council (April 2007) *Single equality scheme: our strategy for equality and diversity*. London: LSC

Websites

Challenging racism: further education leading the way – www.nbm.org.uk/jan06/Commission/cbs_report.pdf

Diverse Voices – http://readingroom.lsc.gov.uk/pre2005/internaladmin/equalitydiversity/diverse-voices.pdf

Human Rights Act – http://tinyurl.com/tmqq9

Equality and Human Rights Commission – www.equalityhumanrights.com/en/yourrights/equalityanddiscrimination/Pages/EqualityHome.aspx

Learning and Skills Council – http://readingroom.lsc.gov.uk/lsc/2005/research/commissioned/through-inclusion-to-excellence.pdf

Learning and Skills Council – http://readingroom.lsc.gov.uk/Lsc/National/nat-singleequalityscheme-30apr07.pdf

Maslow's hierarchy of needs – www.businessballs.com/maslow.htm

Quality Improvement Agency – www.qiaresources4adultlearning.net/

5 REVIEWING YOUR OWN CONTRIBUTION

Introduction

> In this chapter you will learn about:
>
> - interacting with others;
> - sources of information and external agencies;
> - evaluating own practice.

There are activities and examples to help you reflect on the above which will assist your understanding of how to review your own contribution towards promoting equality and diversity in the learning environment.

The appendices contain useful pro-formas you may wish to use.

This chapter contributes towards the following: scope (S), knowledge (K) and practice (P) aspects of the professional standards (A–F domains) for teachers, tutors and trainers in the Lifelong Learning Sector:

AS3, AS4, AS5, AS7;
AK2.1, AK2.2, AK3.1, AK4.2, AK4.3, AK5.1, AK5.2, AK7.3;
AP3.1, AP4.2, AP4.3, AP5.1, AP5.2, AP7.3;
BS2, BS4;
BK1.2, BK2.6, BK2.7, BK3.1, BK3.2, BK3.4;
BP2.7, BP3.4, BP3.5, BP4.1, BP5.2;
CS4;
CK4.2;
CP3.2, CP3.4, CP4.1;
DS1, DS3;
DK1.1, DK2.1, DK3.1, DK3.2;
DP2.1, DP3.2;
ES4;
EK2.1,
FS1, FS2, FS3, FS4;
FK1.1, FK1.2, FK2.1, FK4.2;
FP1.2, FP2.1, FP4.1, FP4.2.

The standards can be accessed at:
www.lluk.org.uk/documents/professional_standards_for_itts_020107.pdf.

Interacting with others

It is important to interact with others, both internal and external to your organisation, to ensure you are being fair to your learners and colleagues. During the interview or induction stages of your programme, you should find out any particular requirements or needs of your learners. If you happen to cover a class for someone else, under the Disability Discrimination Act (DDA) Part Four (1995 amended 2005), the whole organisation is deemed to know. If this information has not been communicated to you, it is wise to ask your learners if there is anything you need to know to help or support them. You might like to encourage your learners to talk to you at the break time or after the session, rather than embarrass them in front of their peers.

Activity

Find out if there is anything you should be aware of regarding your current learners. If there is something that others in your organisation should know, make sure you discuss this with them in a sensitive way, to enable them to support your learners too.

Some things you need to be aware of are learners:

- with varying basic skills such as literacy and numeracy;
- with different learning styles;
- for whom English is not their first language;
- requiring privacy, for example, for prayer, or for taking insulin;
- who are partially deaf or sighted;
- who do not eat during the daylight hours of Ramadan;
- who do not want to eat meat for religious or other reasons;
- who may have to leave early as they have dependants;
- who may not be able to attend all sessions due to work patterns;
- with a physical or mental disability or learning difficulty, for example, Asperger's syndrome, autistic spectrum disorder, etc;
- with dyslexia, dyspraxia, dysgraphia, dyscalculia;
- who may experience financial difficulties.

Finding out anything that may affect your learners or the learning process prior to your teaching will help you plan your session effectively. Taking into account your learners' needs and ensuring you embrace equality and diversity will help to deliver an inclusive session. You may need to liaise with staff within your teaching team or organisation who can give support to your learners. This support could be to help improve skills, for example, literacy and numeracy, or to help learners who are partially sighted or deaf, or any other additional requirements a learner may have. You need to work within the boundaries of your teaching role, don't try to take on any aspects you are not confident or experienced with. There should be staff within your organisation who could advise you of the support arrangements available.

There may be other issues you need to deal with, for example, stereotyping, prejudice and discrimination. If you see anything taking place within your sessions, or hear of anything that could disrupt your sessions, you need to deal with this in a sensitive manner, otherwise the affected learner may lose confidence, not participate during activities or even leave the programme. Communication is the key, not only between you and your learners, but among the group. During the induction stage of your programme, it would be good practice to include a session on the concepts of equality and diversity, highlighting how stereotyping, prejudice and discrimination can affect individuals and groups, and stressing the importance of taking individual responsibility and action to help and support others. This will form a good basis to the beginning of your programme, contribute to the negotiation and setting of ground rules, and hopefully filter through to each learner's home, community and workplace to improve other relationships. Learners will gain increased knowledge, experience and skills from others in the group; they will also feel a sense of acceptance and belonging, and gain respect from others.

Your behaviour can help influence change within your organisation, and that of your learners. Other ways to demonstrate positive behaviour include:

- being fair and consistent with assessment decisions;
- being sympathetic or empathic to learners' problems;
- challenging learners' own attitudes, values and beliefs;
- encouraging and supporting learners to make the best use of their abilities;
- following all legal requirements;
- following all organisational policies and codes of practice;
- making time available to talk to learners about any concerns;
- taking an active interest in learners' interests or problems;
- treating individuals with dignity and respect;
- using a range of activities and resources to promote inclusivity within your sessions.

When communicating, try to use words which support equality and diversity, and encourage your learners to use them too, to prevent any unfair labelling. The table opposite gives some alternative words to use.

Use	Don't use
accessible toilets	disabled toilets
learner with: autistic spectrum disorder, dyslexia, dyspraxia, dysgraphia, dyscalculia, etc.	autistic, dyslexic, etc.
black	coloured
cerebral palsy	spastic
disability	handicapped invalid
gay, lesbian or bisexual	queer
gender examples: police officer, chairperson, people power	policeman/policewoman, chairman, manpower
learning difficulties	mentally handicapped has special educational needs
limited speech without speech	dumb
mental health difficulties	disturbed mental thick, stupid, idiot
non-disabled not disabled	normal (implying disability is abnormal)
partially deaf deaf deafened	hearing handicapped
partially sighted blind	visually handicapped
wheelchair user	wheelchair bound
white	not coloured

Activity

See if you can add to the list with more examples of words and phrases that should and shouldn't be used. Also, consider how assumptions of stereotyping come about; for example, nurses are females, doctors are males.

A model regarding unfair treatment is Allport's (1954) scale of prejudice and discrimination. It was devised by psychologist Gordon Allport and shows what happens if unfair treatment is not stopped.

Allport's scale of prejudice goes from 1 to 5:

1 antilocution (name-calling, stereotyping);

2 avoidance (defamation by omission, exclusion);

3 discrimination (refusal of service, denial of opportunity);

4 physical attack (threat of physical violence, murder);

5 extermination (mass assassination, genocide).

Examples of these include the following:

1 Antilocution – a majority group freely makes jokes about a minority group. Speech is in terms of negative stereotypes and negative images, also called hate speech, and is commonly seen as harmless by the majority. Antilocution itself may not be harmful, but it sets the stage for more severe outlets for prejudice.

2 Avoidance – people in a minority group are actively avoided or ignored by members of the majority group. No direct harm may be intended, but harm is done through isolation.

3 Discrimination – a minority group is discriminated against by denying them opportunities and services that the majority group have, putting prejudice into action. Behaviours have the specific goal of harming the minority group by preventing them from achieving their goals. The majority group is actively trying to harm the minority.

4 Physical attack – the majority group vandalise the minority group's possessions or attack individuals, causing harm.

5 Extermination – the majority group seeks to eliminate or exterminate the minority group. When groups act out their prejudice with physical violence, the way is prepared for directing that energy methodically. In extreme circumstances this can lead to war.

You may experience some of these stages within your groups, perhaps to a lesser degree, or have witnessed things happening within the community or society where you live or work. They shouldn't be ignored. However, you may not feel experienced enough to deal with some issues, therefore you will need to seek the help of others before things get too severe and progress through the scale, putting people at risk of harm.

You might not have experienced many equality and diversity issues within your teaching sessions; however, all your learners will benefit from a discussion or a workshop to increase their awareness. Or it could be the opposite in that you experience issues regularly. The term *ethnic minority*, i.e. a national or racial group living in a country or area which contains a larger group of people of a different race or nationality, may be reversed in favour of the majority. There could be an ethnic majority where you teach. The demographic make-up of the country is very different now to what it was even just a few years ago. You may teach in an area of the country where the majority of your learners are immigrants, therefore the minority are those born in this country. Alternatively, you may teach in an area where the population may be small and therefore not very diverse.

Example

Linda had been asked to analyse some statistics regarding her groups of learners for the past academic year. Besides retention and achievement, this includes gender, age range and ethnic minorities. Linda's organisation is based in a small town, and the only ethnic minority group was the family who owned and worked in the local Chinese restaurant. Her subject of beauty therapy tended to attract females who had recently left school. All of her learners were female aged 16–19 and white. Her external verifier had asked her what she was doing to recruit males and those from ethnic minority groups.

In this situation, it would be difficult for the organisation to recruit learners from ethnic minorities. A way of recruiting males would be by visiting the local school to promote the programme to both males and females, and producing leaflets and posters which included pictures of males as well as females.

If you feel your group does not represent society locally, regionally or nationally, this does not mean you are not differentiating for your learners. You will have individuals who are all different in some way, for example, a single mother who may need to arrange childcare, a learner with dyslexia who prefers handouts on coloured paper, or a learner who lacks confidence as they were bullied at school. Supporting your learners with their individual requirements will help create an encouraging learning environment.

Some people may not have a positive attitude, or be prepared to challenge their own or others' attitudes, values and beliefs. People may try to justify their actions without basing these on facts, or may have inherited negative attitudes. It may take time to change this, but, as a teacher, you can make a difference to people's lives by embracing the diverse nature of your learners and encouraging their individuality.

Sources of information and external agencies

Many organisations are dedicated to the promotion of equality and diversity, and produce useful information, books, leaflets, videos, magazines and other resources. Your own organisation should be proactive and have policies and procedures in place, with information available for staff and learners. By now, you should have found out what is available to you, but you may need to research further for any specific information that could help you and your learners.

The following are details of some of the many organisations that have useful information and/or resources regarding equality and diversity. Each has a website for further information.

- Advice, Conciliation and Arbitration Service – www.acas.org.uk – aims to improve organisations and working life through better employment relations. It helps with employment relations by supplying up-to-date information, independent advice and high-quality training, and working with employers and employees to solve problems and improve performance.

- Audit Commission – www.audit-commission.gov.uk – an independent watchdog, driving economy, efficiency and effectiveness in local public services to deliver better outcomes for everyone.

- Centre for Equality and Diversity – www.cfed.org.uk – a registered charity promoting the interest of all black and minority communities.

- Chartered Institute of Personnel and Development – www.cipd.co.uk – the professional body for those involved in the management and development of people.

- Department for Innovation, Universities and Skills – www.dius.gov.uk – DIUS works with partners from the commercial, public and voluntary sectors to accelerate the commercial exploitation of creativity and knowledge, through innovation and research, to create wealth, grow the economy, build successful businesses and improve quality of life.

- Directgov – www.direct.gov.uk – easy access to information and public services from the UK government.

- Equality and Diversity Forum – www.edf.org.uk – a network of national organisations committed to progress on age, disability, gender, race, religion and belief, sexual orientation and broader equality and human rights issues. It was established in January 2002 to promote dialogue and understanding across the separate equality strands, and to ensure that policy debate on proposals for discrimination legislation and a single equality body recognises the cross-cutting nature of equality issues.

- Equality and Diversity UK – www.inclusive-learning.co.uk – various resources for purchase, information, publications and statistics to improve understanding of issues relating to equality and diversity.

- Equality and Human Rights Commission – www.equalityhumanrights.com – champions equality and human rights for all, working to eliminate discrimination, reduce inequality, protect human rights and to build good relations, ensuring that everyone has a fair chance to participate in society.

- Fire and Rescue Service – www.communities.gov.uk/fire/working/equal opportunities – the *Equality and Diversity Strategy's* vision is to create, by 2018, a service which can demonstrate that it serves all communities equally to the highest standards, building on a closer and more effective relationship with the public and creating a more diverse workforce which better reflects the diversity of the local working population in each area.

- Government Equalities Office – www.equalities.gov.uk – responsible for the government's overall strategy and priorities on equality issues. This includes the Discrimination Law Review, the Single Equality Bill, and the Equality Public Service Agreement.

- Higher Education Funding Council for England – www.hefce.ac.uk – committed to promoting equality and diversity within the staff and learner bodies in higher education.

- Her Majesty's Prison Service – www.hmprisonservice.gov.uk – the Prison Service is committed to promoting equality of opportunity in all its work. The Service operates in an increasingly diverse society. Tackling discrimination of any kind is one of the key priorities for the Service, and forming part of the wider decency agenda, which is essential for the running of a safe and successful Prison Service.

- Improvement and Development Agency for local government – www.idea.gov.uk – the IDeA belongs to local government and leads local government improvement. The Equalities and Cohesion team at the IDeA helps councils to build equality into their core business planning and respond positively to challenges that new legislation brings.

- Investors in People – www.investorsinpeople.co.uk – provides straightforward, proven frameworks for delivering business improvement through people. Information regarding key legislation, leading campaigners, business improvement and good practice tips regarding racial equality in the workplace are available on the site.

- Law Society of Scotland – www.lawscot.org.uk – the Society promotes the interests of the solicitors' profession in Scotland and the interests of the public in relation to the profession.

- Learning and Skills Council – ww.lsc.gov.uk – the LSC exists to make England better skilled and more competitive. Its vision is that, by 2010, *young people and adults in England will have knowledge and skills matching the best in the world and be part of a truly competitive workforce.* It is sure this can be achieved through a strong commitment to equality and diversity.

- Lifelong Learning UK – www.lluk.org/3064.htm – lots of useful links and a range of downloadable resources to help increase knowledge and understanding of current race and ethnicity issues facing the Lifelong Learning Sector.

- MIND – www.mind.org.uk – a charity to advance the views, needs and ambitions of people with experience of mental distress, promote inclusion by challenging discrimination, influence policy through campaigning and education and inspire the development of quality services which reflect expressed need and diversity.

- Ministry of Defence – www.mod.uk – useful information regarding equality and diversity in the Royal Navy, Royal Air Force and British Army.

- National Health Service – www.nhsemployers.org – equality and diversity are at the heart of the NHS strategy. NHS employers' equality and diversity team offers advice, assistance and support to NHS organisations.

- National Institute for Adult Continuing Education – www.niace.org.uk – exists to encourage more and different adults to engage in learning of all kinds. It campaigns for and celebrates the achievements of adult learners, young and old, and in all their diversity. NIACE is the largest organisation working to promote the interests of learners and potential learners in England and Wales.

- Police – www.police.homeoffice.gov.uk – all of the police-related information, support and guidance published by the Home Office, useful to all ranks of serving police officers and anyone involved in the world of policing and justice.

- Post Compulsory Education and Training Network – www.pcet.net – a dedicated, UK-based, further education website which has been designed to support further education teachers from all subject disciplines.

- Qualifications and Curriculum Authority – www.qca.org.uk – maintains and develops the National Curriculum and associated assessments, tests and examinations.

- Quality Improvement Agency – http://excellence.qia.org.uk – an online portal for staff in the further education and skills sector, free resources to support teaching and learning.

- Royal Mail Group – www.royalmailgroup.com – articles and reports, interviews and features to do with diversity at Royal Mail Group and beyond.

- Scottish Disability Team – www.sdt.ac.uk – free resources relating to equality and diversity, funded by the Scottish Funding Council (SFC) and based in the School of Computing at the University of Dundee.

- Stonewall – www.stonewall.org.uk – equality and justice for lesbians, gay men and bisexuals.

- Support for Learning – www.support4learning.org.uk – exists as a signpost to relevant organisations and resources in a number of key areas. The site contains links to resources for advisors, learners and everyone involved in education, training and communities.

- The British Council – www.britishcouncil.org – an international organisation working in over 100 different countries contending with complex equality and diversity issues.

- The Learning and Skills Network – www.lsneducation.org.uk – an independent not-for-profit organisation committed to making a difference to education and training. It aims to deliver quality improvement and staff development programmes that support specific government initiatives, through research, training and consultancy; and by supplying services directly to schools, colleges and training organisations.

- The Royal Society – www.royalsociety.org – the UK's academy of science, which seeks to play an important role in helping to ensure that the UK is maximising the opportunity for all of the population to contribute to the development of science, engineering and technology. The Royal Society believes that UK science would benefit from a more diverse and inclusive culture.

- The Working Group – www.theworkinggroup.org – a non-profit media company that combines television, internet and web resources in the areas of workplace issues; race, diversity and the battle against intolerance; and encouraging democracy and citizen participation.

- Times Educational Supplement online – www.tes.co.uk/resources – free resources produced by teachers, for schools and post-16 learners.

- UNICEF – www.unicef.org.uk – education resources and information.

Activity

Carry out a search via the internet for 'equality and diversity'. See what other organisations there are that you could access to gain further information and useful resources. You may be surprised at just how much information is available, from a wide variety of organisations, groups and associations.

If you come across any useful activities, try these out yourself, and if you feel they are appropriate, encourage your learners to use them.

There are many external agencies or people you will come in to contact with as part of your teaching role. These include:

- Awarding/Examining bodies, for example, external verifiers and moderators;

- careers advisors, job centre staff;

- employers, parents and carers;

- inspectors, for example, from the Office for Standards in Education, Children's Services and Skills;

- schools, colleges, universities and training organisation staff;

- stakeholders, for example, funding bodies such as the Learning and Skills Council (LSC) and local education authorities (LEAs), and partners, for example, voluntary and community groups.

Working with other agencies can help promote equality and diversity within your organisation. There may be experienced and knowledgeable people who are willing to come to your organisation and give talks to your learners, or you could access them for information and resources, or to help improve your knowledge. You could also encourage extracurricular activities for your learners to partake in, for example, joining local societies or clubs.

Whenever you need to communicate with anyone outside of your organisation, remember that you are its representative, and your own attitude may be taken as an extension of the attitude of the organisation. Therefore it is important to remain professional at all times.

The need for awareness extends beyond yourself, the teaching staff and your own learners, to others who give support, for example, caretakers, canteen staff, learning resource staff, volunteers, etc. The management of your organisation and relevant boards of governors should also be proactive in promoting equality and diversity. The recruitment, selection, teaching, support, assessment and review of learners and staff should always be based on potential and ability.

The Centre for Excellence in Leadership's (CEL) first conference dedicated to looking at equality and diversity issues in the further education and skills sector took place in May 2008. Speakers called on all sector leaders to raise the discourse about equality and diversity in their organisations and to model and embed positive values for the benefit of all staff and learners.

Wally Brown CBE, principal of Liverpool Community College, stated:

> An organisation cannot be excellent if it does not embrace equality and diversity 100 per cent – it cannot perform, its staff can't flourish and its learners can't learn. These steps to excellence start with the chair, who seeks out leaders with the right qualities – leaders who embrace equality and lead from the front, keeping us focused. Everyone is responsible for equality and diversity; everyone should take the lead.

The Hon. Lord (Bill) Morris stated:

> Laws alone cannot define equality and diversity; they simply give us the tools to influence behaviour and highlight the opportunity cost. There is a moral and economic case for equality and diversity, and failure to deal with it leads to demotivation, devaluation and discrimination.

The CEL has carried out research into the position of black and minority ethnic (BME) staff in colleges. An executive summary of their document *Succession planning and racial equality in the further education system* can be downloaded from the CEL's website via the internet shortcut http://tinyurl.com/4lyn52.

Evaluating your own practice

When evaluating your own practice, you need to consider how your own behaviour has impacted upon your learners. If you are proactive and have a positive approach, you may still need to challenge your own attitudes, values and beliefs, to ensure you accept and respect others. Your organisation may have a culture of embracing equality and diversity issues, or it may not. If not, you may need to do something about this, to ensure other staff as well as yourself are treating all learners with respect and understanding.

Activity

Think about the way you act with your learners. Answer the following questions honestly, and then consider carefully how you could address any negative responses.

Do you use eye contact with all your learners?

Do you have a favourite learner to whom you give more attention?

Do you ask questions to everyone in the group, or just a few?

Do you discriminate in any way – directly or indirectly?

Do you make any prejudicial or offensive comments towards any learners?

Do you ignore or embarrass learners for any reason?

Do you touch your learners in a way that could be construed as inappropriate?

Do you ensure your teaching methods and resources are accessible to all your learners?

Perhaps you used a handout which didn't reflect different cultures, or a learner had difficulty understanding some jargon you had used. You might have had a learner with a physical difficulty who struggled to access some equipment, or couldn't take part in an activity. You might have a learner who really excels, and you unconsciously give them more praise and encouragement than others. You might even have wanted to impose your own values and beliefs on others, for example, if you didn't agree with something a learner said. If you felt there were some issues, try to plan ahead in future to create a more inclusive environment for all your learners. You could use the checklist in Appendix 4 to help you with your planning and teaching.

Activity

Think about what has contributed to your own attitudes, values and beliefs. Have you managed to formulate your own opinions regarding equality and diversity, or do you feel you have been influenced by others, the organisation within which you work or your family, community and society?

Various factors may have contributed: for example, your upbringing and home life, attitudes of parents or guardians, the influence of colleagues, the culture at previous organisations, or friends and family. You need to realise what has influenced you, to help you make your own opinions, and to consider and respect others. Various issues will arise during your sessions; there will be different interactions between yourself and your learners, and between the learners in your group, which may create awkward situations. Being proactive, and developing an understanding of the differences of your learners is much better than reacting to a situation after it has happened. If you feel the problems have arisen due to a lack of knowledge on the part of your learners, you could carry out an awareness raising session with your group, to help them realise the impact that equality and diversity have on others. If you felt you hadn't prepared adequately, or had an issue that you couldn't satisfactorily resolve, it might be an idea to attend a training session. It is possible your organisation will encourage its staff to embrace equality and diversity issues and provide regular training, or you may be able to attend a programme elsewhere. Your organisation may have an appraisal process, and this would be a good opportunity for you to discuss any areas you don't feel confident with, in order to improve. You may also receive feedback from your line manager or others within your organisation, who may observe your sessions to ensure you are teaching effectively. External inspectors or Awarding/Examining body personnel may also observe your teaching or assessment practice to ensure you are being fair to all learners. If you receive any negative feedback, don't take this personally, but look at *why* this was, and ask *what* you could do to improve for the future.

Example

Aisha is a part-time teacher, covering for an absent member of staff for six weeks. She has a group of learners who are taking a cookery programme and is being observed by her curriculum manager. During the session, she asked the group to plan a main meal for four people of either roast beef or roast pork with vegetables and potatoes, which they would cook during the next week's session. Two learners in the group looked at each other and mumbled, but didn't say anything to Aisha. Throughout the remainder of the session, they whispered among themselves but Aisha didn't do anything about this, even though it became disruptive to the others. During the manager's feedback to Aisha, he asked her if any of her learners were Muslim, Hindu or vegetarian, to which Aisha replied she didn't know. He recommended she follow this up with her learners, and take further training to help improve her knowledge. He also recommended she deal with any disruption when it arises, and offer alternative menu choices to ensure all learners would be included.

Attending training should be a part of your continuing professional development (CPD). Taking the equality and diversity unit of the Professional Teaching Qualifications will help you contribute towards this, as well as improving your knowledge and skills.

Activity

Think about the areas you feel you need to develop regarding equality and diversity. Use the personal development plan in Appendix 6 to consider any training needs you might have, and how you could address these. Follow this up by talking to someone at your organisation who could help, perhaps your mentor or someone from the human resources department.

Keeping your personal development plan up to date, in conjunction with your CPD (sample pro-forma available in Appendix 7) will ensure you can evidence the Institute for Learning's requirement of ongoing CPD. You can update your CPD via the IfL website (www.ifl.ac.uk); by now you should have registered as a member and you will have access to a wealth of information regarding ways to maintain your CPD.

There is continual change in our population, the European Union is growing, and there are major global transformations taking place. You therefore need to keep up to date with changes and developments. There is often debate about what it means to be British, which focuses on religion, culture-related beliefs and dress, which can impact on learning and community cohesion. Legislation needs to be followed, as well as your organisation's own policies and procedures; you therefore need to remain current with your knowledge and practice. After each session you teach, reflect upon what went well, and what you need to change for the future. A straightforward method of reflection is to have the experience, then describe it, analyse it and revise it (EDAR). This method should help you think about what has happened and then consider ways of changing and/or improving it.

Experience → Describe → Analyse → Revise

(Gravells and Simpson, 2008)

- *Experience* – a significant event or incident you would like to change or improve.

- *Describe* – aspects such as who was involved, what happened, when it happened and where it happened.

- *Analyse* – consider the experience deeper and ask yourself how it happened and why it happened.

- *Revise* – think about how you would do it differently if it happened again and then try this out if you have the opportunity.

A way of getting in the habit of reflective practice is to complete an ongoing journal; however, try not to write it like a diary with a description of events, but use EDAR to reflect upon the event.

Activity

Use the reflective learning journal pro-forma in Appendix 8 to reflect upon the last session you taught, using EDAR to help you. Did you have any issues with your learners, or your teaching, for example, discrimination, stereotyping or prejudice? If you did, what could you do to stop this happening again?

You may see your own skills developing, for example, becoming more diplomatic, sensitive, tolerant and respectful to others. Evaluating yourself, your teaching and your group's learning will help to improve your practice in the future. You might identify issues or problems that can be overcome regarding equality and diversity, for example, by producing handouts with different font sizes or colours, not using gender bias when talking, and moving furniture to make the room accessible. However, be careful not to overdo things by indulging the minority to the detriment of the majority.

Feedback from learners is always useful to help you evaluate your teaching and your group's learning. Encouraging learners to talk to you about anything you can do to help them, or things you can change to support their learning, will help build a climate of trust and respect. Never make assumptions that the programme is going well, just because you think it is. Learners may be embarrassed to talk in front of their peers, but unless you know of any issues that may affect them, you can't fully support them.

Besides encouraging informal feedback and discussions, you can gain formal feedback from your learners by issuing questionnaires. Your organisation may have standard ones you are required to use, or you could design your own.

When designing questionnaires, you need to be careful of the type of questions you are using, and consider why you are asking them. Don't just ask questions for the sake of issuing a questionnaire; consider what you really want to find out. When writing questions, gauge the language and complexity to suit your learners, and the types of responses you require to aid analysis. Will your questions be closed, i.e. a question only requiring a yes or no answer; will they be multiple-choice, enabling the learner to choose one or more responses to a question; or will they be open, leading to detailed responses? Questions eliciting responses which can be totalled up are known as *quantitative*; those eliciting a detailed response are known as *qualitative*. Whichever way you gain responses and feedback, make sure you do something with them, to help improve your practice and the support you give your learners.

Reflecting upon your own teaching and taking account of feedback from your learners and colleagues will enable you to become an effective and professional teacher. Ensuring you embrace equality and diversity within the teaching and learning process will help motivate and encourage your learners, promoting a climate of tolerance, trust, respect and achievement.

Summary

In this chapter you have learnt about:

- interacting with others;
- sources of information and external agencies;
- evaluating own practice.

References and further information

Allport, GW (1954) *The nature of prejudice*. Reading, MA: Addison-Wesley

CEL (2008) *Succession planning and racial equality in the further education system*. London: Centre for Excellence in Leadership

Clements, P and Jones, J (2005) *The diversity training handbook: a practical guide to understanding and changing attitudes*. London: Kogan Page

Clements, P and Spinks, T (2005) *The equal opportunities handbook*. London: Kogan Page

Gravells, A and Simpson, S (2008) *Planning and enabling learning*. Exeter: Learning Matters

Websites

Adult Dyslexia Organisation – www.adult-dyslexia.org

Disability Discrimination Act – http://tinyurl.com/2vzd5j (shortcut) or http://www.direct.gov.uk/en/DisabledPeople/RightsAndObligations/DisabilityRights/DG_400 1068

Equality and Diversity Forum – www.edf.org.uk

Institute for Learning – www.ifl.ac.uk

6 RELEVANT LEGISLATION AND REGULATIONS

Introduction

In this chapter you will learn about the:

- Children Act 2004;

- Civil Partnership Act 2004;

- Disability Discrimination Act 1995 (Amendment 2005);

- Disability Rights Commission Act 1999;

- Employment Equality (Age) Regulations 2006;

- Employment Equality (Religion or Belief) Regulations 2003;

- Employment Equality (Sexual Orientation) Regulations 2003;

- Equal Pay Act 1970;

- Equality Act 2006;

- European Union Employment Directive 2000;

- Human Rights Act 1998;

- Protection from Harassment Act 1997;

- Race Relations Act 1976 (Amendment Act 2000 and Amendment Regulations 2003);

- Rehabilitation of Offenders Act 1974;

- Sex Discrimination Act 1975 (Amendment Regulations 2008);

- The Sex Discrimination (Gender Reassignment) Regulations 1999 and the Gender Recognition Act 2004;

- Special Educational Needs and Disability Act 2001;

- Statutory Code of Practice on Racial Equality in Employment 2006;

- Work and Families Act 2006.

There are activities and examples to help you reflect on the above which will assist your understanding of the legislation and regulations surrounding equality and diversity.

This chapter contributes towards the following: scope (S), knowledge (K) and practice (P) aspects of the professional standards (A–F domains) for teachers, tutors and trainers in the Lifelong Learning Sector:

AS1, AS2, AS3, AS4, AS5, AS6, AS7;
AK3.1, AK6.1, AK6.2;
AP5.1, AP5.2, AP6.1, AP6.2;
BK4.1;
BP3.5, BP4.1;
DS1;
FS2, FS4;
FK1.1; FK2.1, FK4.1, FK4.2;
FP1.1, FP2.1, FP4.1, FP4.2.

The standards can be accessed at:
www.lluk.org.uk/documents/professional_standards_for_itts_020107.pdf.

There is a vast amount of legislation currently available which relates to equality and diversity. Not all could be covered comprehensively within this book, therefore this chapter gives a brief overview of those which are most relevant. The information does not constitute legal advice and any errors or omissions are unintentional.

Depending upon whether you work in England, Scotland, Wales or Northern Ireland, there may be some differences from what is stated here, and you are therefore advised to check the current legislation for the nation within which you work. Most legislation is subject to change; therefore you are also advised to check for any relevant updates or amendments which may have taken place since this book was written.

A search via the internet will soon help you locate further details of each Act or Regulation; a useful internet shortcut link has been created and is listed at the end of each section, with other relevant websites listed at the end of the chapter.

Children Act 2004

The Children Act 2004 provides the legal underpinning for the Every Child Matters: Change for Children programme. *Well-being* is the term used in the Act to define the five Every Child Matters outcomes:

- be healthy;

- stay safe;

- enjoy and achieve;

- make a positive contribution;

- achieve economic well-being.

Further details regarding the five outcomes can be located at: www.qca. org.uk/qca_15299.aspx.

Local authorities and their relevant partners must co-operate to improve children's well-being. They must focus on improving outcomes for all children and young people through *children's trusts*, which bring together all services for children and young people in an area. They will support those who work every day with children, young people and their families to deliver better outcomes. This should lead to children and young people experiencing more integrated and responsive services with specialist support. Staff will work in multidisciplinary teams, be trained jointly to tackle cultural and professional divides, and be co-located in extended schools or children's centres.

A key element in the implementation of children's trusts is the development of a strategic plan by the local authority and its partners – the *Children and Young People's Plan*.

The establishment of a Local Safeguarding Children's Board Guidance (LSCB) is an important element of the improved safeguards for children. The LSCB and its activities are part of the wider context of the children's trust arrangements.

Working together to safeguard children: a guide to inter-agency working to safeguard and promote the welfare of children produced by HM Government (2006) sets out how individuals and organisations should work together to safeguard and promote the welfare of children. The guidance has been updated since the previous version, which was published in 1999. The new version reflects developments in legislation, policy and practice. It is aimed at practitioners and front-line managers who have particular responsibilities for safeguarding and promoting the welfare of children, and to senior and operational managers. A copy can be accessed at the Government website via the internet shortcut http://tinyurl.com/3dzztv.

Activity

Find out if you are likely to be affected by the contents of the Children Act 2004. It could be that you teach learners who are under 16 years of age, or vulnerable young people and adults.

Further information can be found at the Department for Children, Schools and Families website via the internet shortcut http://tinyurl.com/3w8mov.

Civil Partnership Act 2004

The Civil Partnership Act 2004 grants legal status to same-sex couples in the United Kingdom and extends the Sex Discrimination Act (1975) to protect them against discrimination. The Act came into force on 5 December 2005, allowing same-sex couples to form civil partnerships. The Act also places cohabiting same-sex couples on the same legal basis as cohabiting heterosexual couples.

Further information can be found at the Directgov website via the internet shortcut http://tinyurl.com/3erj7z.

Disability Discrimination Act 1995 (Amendment 2005)

The Disability Discrimination Act 1995 (DDA) was passed to protect disabled people from discrimination. According to the DDA, *a person has a disability if he or she has a physical or mental impairment, which has a substantial and long-term adverse effect on his/her ability to carry out normal day to day activities.*

The DDA protects disabled people not only in the areas of employment and education, but also in land and property acquisition, and access to goods, facilities and services. It is against the law for employers to discriminate against a disabled person because of their disability:

- by deciding who is offered the job, for example, in the way the applications are handled, the way the interview is carried out or through tests used;

- in the terms on which they offer a job, for example, by just giving a short-term contract;

- by refusing or omitting to offer a job.

When originally released, the DDA contained the following sections:

- Part 1 defined disability;

- Part 2 outlawed discrimination in employment;

- Part 3 outlawed discrimination in other areas of service provision.

In September 2002 the Act was extended to education, which broadened the rights of disabled people. The governing bodies of further education colleges and local education authorities (LEAs) providing adult education are named as responsible bodies which have duties under the legislation. The Special Educational Needs and Disability Act (2001), known as SENDA or Part 4, (see page 94), was an amendment to the DDA, designed to bring education within its remit, ensuring colleges and LEAs have legal responsibilities:

- not to treat disabled learners less favourably for reasons related to their disability;

- to provide reasonable adjustments for disabled learners.

Colleges and LEAs need to anticipate the likely needs of disabled learners and not merely respond to individual needs as they arise. The Act uses a wide definition of disabled person to include: *people with physical or sensory impairments, dyslexia, medical conditions, mental health difficulties and learning difficulties*. Educational organisations have a duty to take reasonable steps to encourage learners to disclose a disability. This could be part of the application or interview stage when a learner commences with your organisation. This encouragement should be ongoing throughout the programme, in case something occurs which may affect a learner's progress.

From 2005 the Act gave disabled people rights in the areas of:

- employment;
- education;
- access to goods, facilities and services;
- buying or renting land or property, including making it easier for disabled people to rent property and for tenants to make disability-related adaptations.

If a learner does disclose a disability or additional need to one person, including you as their teacher, then under the Disability Discrimination Act (DDA) Part Four (1995, amended 2005) the whole organisation is deemed to know. It is therefore important that any issues are communicated to all concerned, and acted upon.

From 2005, organisations have had to make reasonable adjustments to the physical features of their premises to overcome physical barriers to access. When deciding what is reasonable, how much a change will cost and how much the change would help a learner will be taken into consideration.

Example

Fatima has a learner, Marie, who uses a wheelchair. Prior to Marie commencing the programme, Fatima checked all the rooms and facilities that Marie would use, to ensure they were accessible. A special desk was ordered which had adjustable legs that could be raised, and a ramp was installed outside one of the rooms. Signage was also made clearer regarding accessible toilet facilities. As Marie would also need access to the library and computer facilities on the second floor, Fatima checked the lift had controls at a suitable height. She also spoke to the support staff to ensure Marie could access books and computing equipment.

You can also help your learners by organising your environment to enable ease of access around any obstacles (including other learners' belongings), along corridors, and around internal and external doors. When teaching, ensure you face your learners when speaking to assist anyone hard of hearing, produce clearly printed handouts in a font, size and colour to suit any particular learner requirements or use Braille if required. You may have to arrange additional support for some learners to ensure they are not excluded from any activities, and you may need further training yourself to familiarise yourself with particular learner requirements.

Always ask your learners if there is anything you can do to help make their learning experience a positive one.

Activity

Find out who is responsible within your organisation for arranging or adapting equipment and resources. Talk to them to find out what you would need to do to make a request. It could be that this must be done formally, therefore you would need to allow enough time for actions to take place. You might need to borrow equipment from other departments and there may be a booking system for this.

Further information can be found at the Directgov website via the internet shortcut http://tinyurl.com/2vzd5j.

Disability Rights Commission Act 1999

The Disability Rights Commission Act 1999 led to the establishment of the Disability Rights Commission (DRC) in April 2000. It set out the DRC's statutory duties:

- to work to eliminate discrimination against disabled people;

- to promote equal opportunities for disabled people;

- to encourage good practice in the treatment of disabled people;

- to advise the government on the working of disability legislation – the Disability Discrimination Act (DDA) 1995 and the Disability Rights Commission Act 1999.

This Act has now been superseded by the Equality Act 2006.

Employment Equality (Age) Regulations 2006

The Employment Equality (Age) Regulations 2006 came into force on 1 October 2006. The Regulations (which do not affect the age at which people can claim their state pension) set out to:

- ban age discrimination in terms of recruitment, promotion and training;

- ban unjustified retirement ages of below 65;

- remove the current age limit for unfair dismissal and redundancy rights.

They also introduced:

- a right for employees to request working beyond retirement age and a duty on employers to consider that request;

- a new requirement for employers to give at least six months' notice to employees about their intended retirement date so that individuals can plan better for retirement, and be confident that retirement is not being used as cover for unfair dismissal.

The Regulations apply to employment and vocational training. They prohibit unjustified direct and indirect age discrimination, and all harassment and victimisation on grounds of age.

As well as applying to retirement, the Regulations:

- remove the upper age limit for unfair dismissal and redundancy rights, giving older workers the same rights to claim unfair dismissal or receive a redundancy payment as younger workers, unless there is a genuine retirement;

- allow pay and non-pay benefits to continue which depend on length of service requirements of five years or less, or which recognise and reward loyalty and experience and motivate staff;

- remove the age limits for Statutory Sick Pay, Statutory Maternity Pay, Statutory Adoption Pay and Statutory Paternity Pay, so that the legislation for all four statutory payments applies in exactly the same way to all;

- remove the lower and upper age limits in the statutory redundancy scheme, but leave the current age-banded system in place;

- provide exemptions for many age-based rules in occupational pension schemes.

Activity

Look at the resources you are currently using, or plan to use with your learners. Do they differentiate for learners of all ages? Are they inclusive, i.e. there are references to different age groups in any handouts? Are you reliant on using new technology, which older learners might not be familiar with? Always make sure your resources and activities are inclusive, and cover the six strands of equality: age; disability; gender; race; religion and belief; and sexual orientation.

Further information can be found at the Department for Business, Enterprise and Regulatory Reform website via the internet shortcut http://tinyurl.com/3aegpy.

Employment Equality (Religion or Belief) Regulations 2003

The Employment Equality (Religion or Belief) Regulations 2003 are to protect workers, including those on vocational training programmes, from discriminatory employment practices based on actual or perceived religion, or similar belief defined as *religion, religious belief or similar philosophical belief*.

The Regulations make illegal:

- direct discrimination – treating people less favourably than others on the grounds of their religion or belief;

- indirect discrimination – applying a provision, criterion or practice which disadvantages people of a particular religion or belief which is not justified as a proportionate means of achieving a legitimate aim;

- harassment – unwanted conduct that violates people's dignity or creates an intimidating, hostile, degrading, humiliating or offensive environment;

- victimisation – treating people less favourably because of something they have done under, or in connection with, the Regulations, for example, made a formal complaint of discrimination or given evidence in a tribunal case.

The legislation therefore means that schools and colleges:

- cannot refuse access to training, or to promotion, on the basis of religion or belief;

- must act to protect employees against bullying or harassment suffered on grounds of religion or belief. The perception of the person suffering the harassment is crucial;

- cannot deny workers benefits, facilities and services that they offer to other employees, for example, insurance schemes, travel concessions or social events on the basis of religion or belief;

- cannot give an unfair reference when someone leaves because of their religion or belief.

Example

Jack was reviewing applications from prospective learners for a one-week's Exercise to Music programme. The maximum number he could take was 12, but he had 16 applicants. Four of these were Muslim; Jack therefore decided he would not accept them as he did not want to offend them. He was concerned they would complain about the dress code, and that they would not attend at various times because they would want to pray.

In this example, Jack was directly discriminating against the four Muslim applicants and therefore breaking the law.

Further information can be found at the Teachers' Union website via the internet shortcut http://tinyurl.com/4bnmry.

Employment Equality (Sexual Orientation) Regulations 2003

The Employment Equality (Sexual Orientation) Regulations 2003 are to protect workers, including those on vocational training programmes, from discriminatory employment practices based on actual or perceived sexual orientation defined as *heterosexual, gay, lesbian or bisexual.*

The Regulations make illegal:

- direct discrimination – treating people less favourably than others on grounds of their sexual orientation;

- indirect discrimination – applying a provision, criterion or practice which disadvantages people of a particular sexual orientation which is not justified as a proportionate means of achieving a legitimate aim;

- harassment – unwanted conduct that violates people's dignity or creates an intimidating, hostile, degrading, humiliating or offensive environment;

- victimisation – treating people less favourably because of something they have done under, or in connection with, the Regulations, for example, made a formal complaint of discrimination or given evidence in a tribunal case.

Example

Fiona complained to her teacher that she was being harassed by a couple of other learners in the group. She had recently informed her peers she was a lesbian and felt this was the reason why. Rather than embarrass Fiona or draw attention to the learners in question, her teacher amended her next session plan to include a discussion about equality and diversity. The harassment stopped once the learners had gained a better understanding of how to embrace people's differences.

Further information can be found at the Department for Business, Enterprise and Regulatory Reform website via the internet shortcut http://tinyurl.com/4nqrnh.

Equal Pay Act 1970

The Equal Pay Act 1970 was introduced to eliminate discrimination between men and women in terms of their pay and contracts of employment. This relates to:

- work that is the same or broadly similar;

- work rated as equivalent under a job evaluation study;

- work of equal value in terms of the demands made on them under headings such as effort, skill and decision-making.

The Equal Pay Act gives men and women the right to equality in the terms of their contract of employment. It covers pay and other terms and conditions such as piecework, output and bonus payments, holidays and sick leave.

European law has extended the concept of equal pay to include redundancy payments, travel concessions, employers' pension contributions and occupational pension benefits. This means that even though a man and a woman are receiving the same basic rate of pay, there may still be a breach of the principle of equal pay because other benefits (such as a company car, private health care, etc.) are not provided on an equal basis.

The Act relates to pay or benefits provided by a contract of employment, and applies to all employers irrespective of their size, and whether they are in the public or private sector.

Further information can be found at the Government Equalities' Office website via the internet shortcut http://tinyurl.com/5ytphb.

Equality Act 2006

The Equality Act 2006 replaced the Equal Opportunities Commission (EOC), the Commission for Racial Equality (CRE) and the Disability Rights Commission (DRC) with the Commission for Equality and Human Rights (CEHR).

The Equality and Human Rights Commission champions equality and human rights for all, working to eliminate discrimination, reduce inequality, protect human rights and to build good relations, ensuring that everyone has a fair chance to participate in society.
(http://www.equalityhumanrights.com/en/Pages/default.aspx)

The EOC has called the Act *the most significant change in gender equality legislation for 30 years.* All public-sector bodies will have a general duty in the exercise of their public functions to pay due regard to the need to eliminate unlawful discrimination, and to promote equality between men and women, known as the Gender Equality Duty (GED).

The Act has four main purposes. These are:

- to establish the Commission for Equality and Human Rights to cover England, Scotland and Wales;

- to make unlawful discrimination on the grounds of religion or belief in the provision of goods, facilities and services, premises, education, and the exercise of public functions;

- to create a duty on public authorities to promote equality of opportunity between women and men (the Gender Equality Duty), and to prohibit sex discrimination in the exercise of public functions;

- to allow regulations to be made prohibiting discrimination on grounds of sexual orientation in the provision of goods, facilities and services.

The CEHR will be responsible for promoting understanding of equality and human rights issues and for challenging unlawful discrimination. It will take over the functions of the Commission for Racial Equality from April 2009. It will also have responsibility for promoting other specific areas of discrimination, for example, sexual orientation, religion or belief and age, and will have a wider general remit to promote human rights and equality generally, even those areas not covered by specific pieces of legislation.

To ensure you comply with the Act, you need to ensure you are proactive in all aspects of equality and diversity, and make sure your teaching delivery and resources are inclusive in respect of the six strands:

- age;
- disability;
- gender;
- race;
- religion and belief;
- sexual orientation.

Activity

Find out if your organisation is actively promoting the Equality Act 2006. Is any information displayed on noticeboards; have you been invited to attend any training sessions? Make sure you are aware of the implications of the six strands, and that your colleagues are too.

Further information can be found at the Government Equalities Office website via the internet shortcut http://tinyurl.com/4uaqoq.

European Union (EU) Employment Directive 2000

The European Employment Directive 2000 put in place a general framework for equal treatment in employment and vocational training and guidance. It is commonly called the EU Directive. It was designed to make discrimination illegal on the grounds of age, disability, gender, race, religion and belief, or sexual orientation.

A directive works by ensuring a European member state passes new legislation in its own country, to meet the required timescales.

The main points of the Employment Directive are that:

- member states commit themselves to take necessary measures to ensure that any laws, regulations, collective agreements, internal rules of organisations or independent occupations are not contrary to the principle of equal treatment;

- it applies to both the public and private sectors, including public bodies;

- it does not affect provisions made by member states governing the entry and residence of third-country nationals (people who have the nationality of a state outside the current EU membership) and their access to employment and occupations;

- the provision of measures to accommodate the needs of disabled people at the workplace are a necessary part of combating discrimination on the grounds of disability;

- member states' armed forces, police, prison and emergency services are exempted, for operational purposes, from the Employment Directive;

- limited exceptions to the principle of equal treatment may be allowed, for example, to preserve the ethos of religious organisations or to allow special schemes to promote the integration of older or younger workers into the labour market;

- for the principle of equal treatment to be applied effectively, the burden of proof must shift back to the respondent when evidence of such discrimination is brought;

- member states are expected to promote dialogue between the social partners (employers, labour unions and non-governmental organisations) to combat discrimination in the workplace.

The Employment Directive lays down the minimum requirements; member states have the option of introducing or maintaining more favourable provisions.

Further information can be found at the Department for Business Enterprise and Regulatory Reform's website via the internet shortcut http://tinyurl.com/4qzjd8.

Human Rights Act 1998

The Human Rights Act 1998 came into force in October 2000. All people should have basic rights, which include:

- the right to life (Article 2);

- freedom from torture or inhuman or degrading treatment (Article 3);

- freedom from slavery or forced labour (Article 4);

- personal freedom (Article 5);

- the right to a fair trial (Article 6);

- no punishment without law (Article 7);

- private life and family (Article 8);

- freedom of belief (Article 9);

- free expression (Article 10);

- free assembly and association (Article 11);

- marriage (Article 12);

- freedom from discrimination (Article 14).

Article 14 of the European Convention on Human Rights states that:

> ... the enjoyment of the rights and freedoms set forth in this Convention shall be secured without discrimination on any grounds such as sex, race, colour, language, religion, political or other opinion, national or social origin, association with a national minority, property, birth or other status.

All public bodies are required to adhere to the Act and the courts must interpret UK law in accordance with the European Convention on Human Rights and Fundamental Freedoms.

To date, Article 11 has not been interpreted by the European Court of Human Rights to entitle employees to time off on religious holidays or days of rest. Article 10 has not been interpreted to give employees the right to wear what they like to work. However, UK law makes discrimination against a person on the basis of their religion or belief illegal.

Article 8 may be of importance where employers interfere with communications by staff, such as intercepting telephone calls, e-mail or interfering with internet use. The disclosure of personal information about an employee to third parties without that employee's consent may breach Article 8, particularly if it is confidential medical information, which is also illegal under Data Protection legislation.

Further information can be found at the Department for Constitutional Affairs' website via the internet shortcut http://tinyurl.com/tmqq9.

Protection from Harassment Act 1997

The Protection from Harassment Act 1997 introduced four new criminal offences:

- harassment: six months' imprisonment and/or a fine;

- fear of violence: five years' imprisonment and/or a fine on indictment;

- breach of civil injunction: five years' imprisonment and/or a fine on indictment;

- breach of restraining order: five years' imprisonment and/or a fine on indictment.

Further information can be found at the Crown Prosecution Service website via the internet shortcut http://tinyurl.com/4flds7.

Race Relations Act 1976 (Amendment Act 2000 and Amendment Regulations 2003)

The Race Relations Act 1976 made it illegal to discriminate on the grounds of:

- colour;

- race;

- nationality (including citizenship);

- ethnic or national origin.

It applies to discrimination in employment and vocational training, education, housing and the provision of goods, facilities and services.

This includes:

- benefits granted by employers;

- choosing successful applicants;

- dismissal, disciplinary hearings;

- opportunities for promotion;

- terms of employment;

- the selection process;

- transfers or training;

- unfair treatment of employees.

Example

Paul was due to take an evening class of 20 adult learners wanting to achieve Advanced level maths. He noticed two names on the list sounded Polish. Paul telephoned them prior the start date, and persuaded them not to attend. He advised them to take a GCSE instead. Paul was concerned that they would not achieve, therefore affecting his retention and achievement rates. In reality, it turned out the prospective learners were English and had a Polish surname by marriage. Paul had made a wrong assumption and broken the law by discriminating.

Further information can be found at the Commission for Racial Equality website via the internet shortcut http://tinyurl.com/4z5ckt.

The Race Relations (Amendment) Act 2000 places a general duty on all public bodies, for example, local councils, schools, colleges and the police force, to:

- eliminate unlawful racial discrimination;

- promote equality of opportunity;

- promote good relations between persons of different racial groups.

Public bodies are required to produce and publish a Race Equality Scheme Action Plan that sets out how they will meet these general duties, for example, through staff training, and monitoring staff and customers by ethnic origin. As part of their duties, public bodies that purchase services or contract with private companies require that the companies they contract with are also compliant with the legislation. They should also have policies and procedures that do not have an adverse impact on one group of people in relation to another.

Further information can be found at the Department for Children, Schools and Families website via the internet shortcut http://tinyurl.com/3p5bvd.

The Race Regulations Act 2003 made changes to the Race Relations Act 1976. The Regulations offer protection on the basis of race, ethnic or national origin, not colour or nationality. The original provisions still apply in relation to colour and nationality. The Regulations bring in new definitions of indirect discrimination, racial harassment and genuine occupational requirement. In many aspects of employment practice, the Regulations mirror the Employment Equality Regulations.

Further information can be found at the Government website via the internet shortcut http://tinyurl.com/3jsw7v.

Rehabilitation of Offenders Act 1974

The Rehabilitation of Offenders Act 1974 came into force in July 1975 (except for Northern Ireland). Anyone who has been convicted of a criminal offence, and received a sentence of not more than two and a half years in prison, will benefit as a result of the Act, providing they are not convicted again during a specified period otherwise known as the rehabilitation period. The length of this period depends on the sentence given for the original offence, and runs from the date of the conviction. If the person does not reoffend during this rehabilitation period, they become a rehabilitated person, and their conviction becomes spent or is ignored.

Sentences can carry fixed or variable rehabilitation periods and these periods can be extended if the person offends again during the rehabilitation period. However, if the sentence is more than two and a half years in prison, the conviction will never be spent. It is the sentence imposed by the courts that counts, even if it is a suspended sentence, not the time actually spent in prison.

Once a conviction is spent, the convicted person does not have to reveal it or admit its existence (in most circumstances). The two main exceptions relate to working with children or working with the elderly or sick people. If a person wants to apply for a position that involves working with children or working with the elderly or sick people, they are required to reveal all convictions, both spent and unspent.

The Criminal Records Bureau (CRB) is an executive agency of the Home Office, which provides access to criminal record information through a disclosure service. If you work with children or vulnerable adults, you will need to provide proof of a CRB check.

Further information can be found at the Criminal Records Bureau website via the internet shortcut http://tinyurl.com/4ccndo.

Sex Discrimination Act 1975 (Amendment Regulations 2008)

The Sex Discrimination Act 1975 made it illegal to discriminate on the grounds of sex in:

- employment and vocational training;
- education;
- housing;
- the provision of goods, facilities and services.

It is also illegal to discriminate on the grounds of marriage in relation to employment provision.

The Sex Discrimination Act 1975 (Amendment) Regulations 2008 are intended to bring the Act into line with the Equal Treatment Directive 1976, which put into effect *the principle of equal treatment for men and women as regards access to employment, including promotion, and to vocational training.*

Further information can be found at the Government Equalities website via the internet shortcut http://tinyurl.com/3fhjjf.

The Sex Discrimination (Gender Reassignment) Regulations 1999 and the Gender Recognition Act 2004

These Regulations extended the Sex Discrimination Act 1975 (SDA) to make it illegal to discriminate on the grounds of gender reassignment, but only in the areas of employment and vocational training. They do not cover the provision of goods, facilities or services. Gender reassignment is defined by the SDA as a process which is undertaken under medical supervision for the purposes of reassigning a person's sex by changing physiological or other characteristics of sex, and includes any part of such a process.

Further information can be found at the Press for Change website via the internet shortcut http://tinyurl.com/6f6762.

The Gender Recognition Act 2004 enables people who meet the requirements of the Act to change their legal gender. This includes the right to a new birth certificate, if the birth was registered in the UK, and provides recognition of a person's acquired gender for all legal purposes. This means that the person must be regarded as their acquired gender in all aspects of life. Under the Act, people who are at least 18 years of age are eligible to formally apply for a Gender Recognition Certificate (GRC) if they have:

- officially changed their name (if necessary);
- been living full-time in their acquired gender for over two years, and intend to do so permanently;
- been diagnosed as having gender dysphoria.

Surgery or any other gender reassignment treatment, such as hormone therapy, are not a prerequisite to obtaining a certificate. Once a person has their GRC, they must be regarded as a member of their acquired gender for all purposes, including legal records. This means that a female-to-male trans man with a GRC can apply for a job where being male is a genuine occupational qualification, for example, as a male care assistant. Knowledge about a person's gender recognition is regarded as protected information. Anyone who acquires such knowledge in the course of their official duties and then passes it on to a third party without the trans person's consent may be prosecuted and fined.

In April 2007, the Forum on Sexual Orientation and Gender Identity in Post-School Education was established, bringing together relevant bodies in further and higher education. Its aim is to co-ordinate work on sexual orientation and gender identity equality, and to share expertise. A document called *Guidance on trans equality in post school education* (2007) has been produced which provides background information, practical advice and examples of best practice, to help post-16 educational establishments take positive steps to fulfil their legal requirements, and provide a positive environment for trans workers and learners.

Activity

Access the website www.unison.org.uk/file/A7002.pdf, and have a look at the Guidance on trans equality in post school education. Reading the contents will increase your knowledge and understanding.

Special Educational Needs and Disability Act 2001

The Special Educational Needs and Disability Act (SENDA) 2001 is often referred to as Part Four of the Disability Discrimination Act (DDA) 1995. SENDA is the part of the DDA that relates to education.

SENDA introduced the right for disabled learners not to be discriminated against in education, training and any services provided wholly or mainly for learners, and for those enrolled on programmes provided by responsible bodies, for example, further and higher education institutions and sixth-form colleges.

Colleges and LEAs have a legal responsibility:

- not to treat disabled learners less favourably for any reason related to their disability;
- to provide reasonable adjustments for disabled learners.

Learner services covered by the Act can include a wide range of educational and non-educational services, for example, field trips, catering facilities, examinations and assessments, arrangements for work placements, libraries and learning resources.

If a disabled person is at a substantial disadvantage, responsible bodies are required to take reasonable steps to prevent that disadvantage. This could include:

- changes to policies and practices;
- changes to programme requirements or work placements;
- changes to the physical features of a building;
- the provision of an interpreter or other support staff;
- the provision of resources in other formats.

The reasonable steps taken will depend upon:

- the type of services being provided;
- the nature of the institution or service and its size and resources;
- the effect of the disability on the individual disabled person or learner.

If necessary, the final decision about what is reasonable will be decided by the courts.

Activity

Find out what you should do to help a learner who discloses to you they have a disability. Also, check your organisation's application forms to ensure a question is asked to enable a prospective learner to inform you of any disability that may affect their learning. Some learners may not consider they have a disability, and therefore not disclose it. It is important to encourage your learners to discuss anything with you that may affect their attendance or the learning process.

Further information can be found at the Directgov website via the internet shortcut http://tinyurl.com/3zkrpr.

Statutory Code of Practice on Racial Equality in Employment 2006

The Statutory Code of Practice on Racial Equality in Employment 2006 replaced the Statutory Code of Practice for the Elimination of Racial Discrimination and the Promotion of Equality of Opportunity in Employment, issued by the Commission for Racial Equality (CRE) in 1984 under the Race Relations Act (RRA) 1976.

It was introduced to help eliminate racism at work. The Code of Practice provides employers with guidance on how to avoid unlawful racial discrimination, and outlines employers' legal obligations under the Race Relations Act. Employment tribunals will take the Code's recommendations into account in any legal proceedings brought on or after 6 April 2006.

The RRA gives the CRE a legal duty to:

- work towards the elimination of racial discrimination and harassment;
- promote equality of opportunity and good relations between people from different racial groups;
- keep under review the way the RRA is working, and, if necessary, make proposals to the Secretary of State for amending it.

Further information can be found at the Home Office website via the internet shortcut http://tinyurl.com/3lt35r.

Work and Families Act 2006

The Work and Families Act 2006 is the first step towards delivery of some of the measures set out in the Government's response to the consultation, *work and families: choice and flexibility*, which was published in 2006. The legislation aims to support both employers and working families by providing a framework of rights and responsibilities for both employer and employee. This includes:

- adoption leave and pay;
- flexible working and work–life balance;
- maternity leave and pay;
- paternity leave and pay;
- additional paternity leave and pay;
- parental leave;
- part-time work;
- time off for dependants.

Further information can be found at the Department for Regulatory Reform's website via the internet shortcut http://tinyurl.com/46prm4

The Department for Innovation, Universities and Skills (DIUS) published a News Release issued by the Government News Network on 14 May 2008 (2008/026) to give a:

- legal right for employees to request time to train;

- legislation to expand and strengthen apprenticeships.

For the first time, employees will be given the legal right to request time to train from their employers, and apprenticeships will receive a boost under new legislation to unlock the potential of individuals and businesses.

The Government will consult on how workers can be legally empowered to request time to undertake training that will benefit them and their employer. By introducing a new right to ask for time for training, employees will be able to talk to employers about their training needs, and employers will become more aware of the public funds available to support training.

Employers will be legally obliged to seriously consider requests for training they receive, but could refuse a request where there was a good business reason to do so. Employers will not be obliged to meet the salary or training costs to enable a request for time to train, but many may choose to do so, recognising the opportunity to invest in their business.

An Education and Skills Bill will underpin the drive to extend opportunity, improve national competitiveness and raise aspirations throughout society.

Further information can be found at the Department for Innovation, Universities and Skills website via the internet shortcut http://tinyurl.com/5uqufu.

Summary

In this chapter you have learnt about the:

- Children Act 2004;

- Civil Partnership Act 2004;

- Disability Discrimination Act 1995 (Amendment 2005);

- Disability Rights Commission Act 1999;

- Employment Equality (Age) Regulations 2006;

- Employment Equality (Religion or Belief) Regulations 2003;

- Employment Equality (Sexual Orientation) Regulations 2003;

- Equal Pay Act 1970;

- Equality Act 2006;

- European Union Employment Directive 2000;

- Human Rights Act 1998;

- Protection from Harassment Act 1997;

- Race Relations Act 1976 (Amendment Act 2000 and Amendment Regulations 2003);

- Rehabilitation of Offenders Act 1974;

- Sex Discrimination Act 1975 (Amendment Regulations 2008);

- The Sex Discrimination (Gender Reassignment) Regulations 1999 and the Gender Recognition Act 2004;

- Special Educational Needs and Disability Act 2001;

- Statutory Code of Practice on Racial Equality in Employment 2006;

- Work and Families Act 2006.

References and further information

HMI (2004) *Every Child Matters: change for children.* London: DfES

HMI (2006) *Working together to safeguard children: a guide to inter-agency working to safeguard and promote the welfare of children.* London: HM Government

Learning and Skills Council (2007) *Equality and diversity – what's that then?* East Midlands: LSC

Press for Change (2007) *Guidance on trans equality in post school education.* London: Unison

Websites

All government legislation and regulations can be found at – www.opsi.gov.uk

Criminal Records Bureau – www.crb.gov.uk

Department for Business, Enterprise and Regulatory Reform – www.berr.gov.uk

Department for Innovation, Universities and Skills – www.dius.gov.uk

Equality and Diversity Forum – www.edf.org.uk

Equality and Human Rights Commission – www.equalityhumanrights.com

Equality for Lesbians, Gay Men and Bisexuals – www.stonewall.org.uk

Every Child Matters – www.everychildmatters.gov.uk

Legal and human rights organisation – www.justice.org.uk

Mental health – www.mind.org.uk

Migrant Workers Gateway – www.migrantgateway.eu

Refugee Council – www.refugeecouncil.org.uk

Shortcut website addresses – www.tinyurl.com

Terence Higgins Trust – www.tht.org.uk

APPENDIX I ABBREVIATIONS AND ACRONYMS

AB – Awarding Body

ACL – Adult and Community Learning

ADS – Adult Dyslexia Support

ALN – Adult Literacy and Numeracy

ATLS – Associate Teacher Learning and Skills

BCoDP – British Council of Disabled People

BIHR – British Institute of Human Rights

BME – Black and Minority Ethnic

BSA – Basic Skills Agency

CEHR – Commission for Equality and Human Rights

CEL – Centre for Excellence in Leadership

CPD – Continuing Professional Development

CRB – Criminal Records Bureau

CRE – Commission for Racial Equality

CTLLS – Certificate in Teaching in the Lifelong Learning Sector

DCFS – Department for Children, Families and Schools

DEE – Disability Equality in Education

DDA – Disability Discrimination Act 1995 (Amendment 2005)

DIUS – Department for Innovation Universities and Skills

DRC – Disability Rights Commission

DTI – Department for Trade and Industry

DTLLS – Diploma in Teaching in the Lifelong Learning Sector

EDF – Equality and Diversity Forum

EOC – Equal Opportunities Commission

ESOL – English for Speakers of Other Languages

GED – Gender Equality Duty

GOQ – Genuine Occupational Qualification

GRC – Gender Recognition Certificate

HEI – Higher Education Institution

HSE – Health and Safety Executive

ICT – Information Communication Technology

IfL – Institute for Learning

ILT – Information Learning Technology

ILP – Individual Learning Plan

IT – Information Technology

LLN – Language, Literacy, Numeracy

LLUK – Lifelong Learning UK

LSC – Learning and Skills Council

LSCB – Local Safeguarding Children Board

LSN – Learning and Skills Network

NEET – Not in Employment, Education or Training

NIACE – National Institute of Adult Continuing Education

NVQ – National Vocational Qualification

OfSTED – Office for Standards in Education, Children's Services and Skills

PCET – Post Compulsory Education and Training

PGCE – Post Graduate Certificate in Education

PTLLS – Preparing to Teach in the Lifelong Learning Sector

QCA – Qualifications and Curriculum Authority

QCF – Qualifications and Credit Framework

QIA – Quality Improvement Agency

QTLS – Qualified Teacher Learning and Skills

RNIB – Royal National Institute for the Blind

RNID – Royal National Institute for the Deaf

SDA – Sex Discrimination Act 1975 (Amendment 2008)

SENDA – Special Educational Needs and Disability Act 2001

SMART – Specific, Measurable, Achievable, Realistic, and Time bound

SVUK – Standards Verification UK

VACSR – Valid, Authentic, Current, Sufficient, Reliable

VARK – Visual, Aural, Read/Write, Kinaesthetic

VYP – Vulnerable Young People

Ability – the power or skill needed to do something, usually physical or mental.

Age – the period of time a person has been living.

Appreciate – to recognise that something is important or valuable.

Attitude – to speak or act in a way that makes values and beliefs very clear to others.

Barrier – anything that prevents people from accessing something, or understanding others.

Behaviour – actions or reactions to situations or circumstances.

Belief – feeling certain that something is true or exists.

Challenge – to question whether something is true, exists or is legal.

Citizen – an inhabitant of a town or city, who may be entitled to some privileges as a result.

Civil ceremony – a non-religious legal partnership between members of the opposite sex.

Civil partnership – a legal partnership between members of the same sex.

Class – a group of people in society who have the same position, for example, social or economic.

Colour – the natural colour of a person's skin by birth.

Culture – the beliefs and customs of a particular group of people.

Dependant – a person who depends on another for support.

Differentiation – the process of recognising something as being different.

Direct discrimination – being treated less favourably than another person in the same situation.

Disability – a condition, illness or injury that makes it difficult for a person to do the same things others can do.

Discrimination – treating a person or group differently, often in a negative manner.

Diverse – different or varied in some way.

Diversity – valuing the individual differences of a person.

Domestic circumstances – belonging to, or relating to, the family house or home.

Dysphoria – an unpleasant or uncomfortable mood, anxiety, irritability, or restlessness, the opposite of euphoria.

Education – the process of teaching or learning.

Employment status – when a person is paid to carry out a relevant job role.

Equal – of the same importance and deserving the same treatment.

Equal opportunity – the principle of treating all people the same.

Equality – enjoying equal rights, being of the same importance and receiving the same treatment. A revised term for equal opportunities and based on the legal obligation to comply with anti-discrimination legislation.

Ethical – something which is morally right.

Ethnic minority – a national or racial group of people living in a country or area which contains a larger group of people of a different nationality or race.

Ethnic origin – where a national or racial group of people were born.

Ex-offender – person with a criminal record or criminal history.

Exclusion – to keep out or omit.

Experience – skills, knowledge and/or attitudes obtained from various activities.

Fair – treating others in a way that is reasonable and right.

Faith – a strong belief, often religious.

Gender – the differences between men and women.

Grievance – a concern, problem or complaint.

Harassment – behaviour likely to annoy or upset another person.

Human rights – the basic rights which it is generally considered all people should have, for example, justice and freedom to speak.

Illegal – prohibited by law or official rules and regulations.

Immigrant – a person who permanently settles in another country after leaving their own.

Inclusive – involving everyone, treating them all equally and fairly, without directly or indirectly excluding anyone.

Indirect discrimination – when there are rules that apply to everyone but affect an individual or group of people more than others, without good reason.

Inequality – a lack of equality or fair treatment between people.

Integration – the process of combining a group of people, for example, a minority group, with members of a majority group.

Intersectional discrimination – treating a person less favourably on more than one ground simultaneously, the grounds not being separated, for example, female and Asian.

Language – a system of communication used by people of a particular country or profession.

Learning difficulties – mental problems which affect a person's ability to learn.

Marital status – whether or not a person is married.

Migrant – a person who moves from one region or area to another.

Minority – a small group of people who are different from the majority.

Modified grievance – a shorter grievance procedure for a person who has left employment.

Moral – behaving in ways considered by most people to be correct and honest.

Multidimensional discrimination – discrimination on more than one ground. The grounds could be separated depending upon the circumstances, for example, age and disability.

National origin – where a person's ancestors come from, for example, a particular country, heritage or background.

Nationality – the official right to belong to a particular country or countries.

Offend – to upset a person or make them angry.

Oppose – to disagree with a person or something.

Others – carers, children, colleagues, employers, family, friends, local community, mentors, parents, partners.

Parental status – the status of one person in respect to another, the other being under the age of 18 (or who is 18 or older but is incapable of self-care because of a physical or mental disability). Examples include a biological parent; an adoptive parent; a foster parent; a step-parent; a legal guardian.

Policy – a set of ideas that has been agreed officially by a group of people.

Political conviction – opinions about how a country should be governed.

Positive discrimination – the practice of giving advantage to those groups in society which are often treated unfairly, usually because of race or sex.

Prejudice – an unfair and unreasonable view or judgement.

Race – a group of people with similar characteristics.

Racism – the character and behaviour which is influenced by a person's race against another race.

Racist – a person who treats other races unfairly, believing they are not as good as their own race.

Reasonable – being fair.

Reasonable adjustments – a legal term introduced under the Disability Discrimination Act 1995. An employer has a duty to make reasonable adjustments where arrangements or physical premises could place a disabled person at a substantial disadvantage to a person who is not disabled.

Recognise – to accept something, based on experience.

Religion – any system of belief and/or worship.

Respect – to accept or admire.

Reverse discrimination – when an advantage is given to people who are typically thought to be treated unfairly, usually because of their race or sex.

Rights – the claim which a person has to be treated in a fair, morally acceptable or legal way.

Sex – being male or female.

Sexual orientation – relating to being male or female.

Social background – a person's family and experiences, for example, education, wealth, living conditions, etc.

Statutory grievance – a three-step procedure all workplaces must have.

Stereotype – a fixed, commonly held notion or image, which is possibly wrong.

Tolerant – accepting of the behaviour and beliefs of others, even if not agreeing or approving of them.

Tradition – principles, beliefs or a way of life which people have followed for a long time.

Transgender or transperson – a person whose identity does not conform to conventional ideas of male or female. It ranges from how a person dresses to a person who has multiple surgical operations to reassign to their preferred gender role.

Unethical – something which is morally wrong.

Unfair – unreasonable or not right.

Value – the importance placed upon a person or something.

Victimisation – unfavourable treatment of a person.

Vulnerable – a person who could easily be hurt, for example, emotionally, physically or mentally.

UNIT TITLE: Equality and diversity level 3 (six credits)

Learning outcomes The learner will:	Assessment criteria The learner can:
1 Understand the key features of a culture which promotes equality and values diversity	1.1 Explain the meaning and benefits of diversity and the promotion of equality 1.2 Explain forms of inequality and discrimination and their impact on individuals, communities and society 1.3 Identify and outline the relevant legislation, employment regulations and policies and codes of practice relevant to the promotion of equality and valuing of diversity
2 Understand the importance of the promotion of equality and valuing of diversity for effective work in the sector	2.1 Explain how the promotion of equality and diversity can protect people from risk of harm 2.2 Explain action taken to value individuals and its impact 2.3 Explain good practice in providing individuals with information
3 Understand and demonstrate behaviour appropriate to the promotion of equality and valuing of diversity	3.1 Explain and demonstrate ways of communication and behaviour which support equality and diversity 3.2 Explain impact of own behaviour on individuals and their experience of the organisation's culture and approach 3.3 Explain how own behaviour can impact on own organisation's culture 3.4 Explain how working with other agencies can promote diversity
4 Understand how to actively help others in the promotion of equality and valuing of diversity	4.1 Describe actions by individuals which can undermine equality and diversity and review strategies for dealing with these effectively 4.2 Explain strategies for dealing with systems and structures which do not promote equality and diversity
5 Understand how to review own contribution to promoting equality and valuing diversity	5.1 Identify own strengths and areas for development in promoting equality and valuing diversity, using reflection and feedback from individuals 5.2 Identify and use appropriate sources for support in promoting equality and valuing diversity, explaining why this is necessary

UNIT TITLE: Equality and diversity level 4 (six credits)

Learning outcomes The learner will:	Assessment criteria The learner can:
1 Understand the key features of a culture which promotes equality and values diversity	1.1 Analyse the meaning and benefits of diversity and the promotion of equality 1.2 Analyse forms of inequality and discrimination and their impact on individuals, communities and society 1.3 Discuss how relevant legislation, employment regulations and policies and codes of practice contribute to the promotion of equality and valuing of diversity
2 Understand the importance of the promotion of equality and valuing of diversity for effective work in the sector	2.1 Discuss how the promotion of equality and diversity can protect people from risk of harm 2.2 Evaluate action taken to value individuals and its impact 2.3 Summarise and demonstrate good practice in providing individuals with information
3 Understand and demonstrate behaviour appropriate to the promotion of equality and valuing of diversity	3.1 Explain and demonstrate ways of communication and behaviour which support equality and diversity 3.2 Analyse impact of own behaviour on individuals and their experience of the organisation's culture and approach 3.3 Review the impact of own behaviour on own organisation's culture 3.4 Explain and demonstrate how working with other agencies can promote diversity
4 Understand how to actively help others in the promotion of equality and valuing of diversity	4.1 Analyse actions by individuals which can undermine equality and diversity and evaluate strategies for dealing with these effectively 4.2 Evaluate strategies for dealing with systems and structures which do not promote equality and diversity
5 Understand how to review own contribution to promoting equality and valuing diversity	5.1 Evaluate own strengths and areas for development in promoting equality and valuing diversity, using reflection and feedback from individuals 5.2 Identify, use and evaluate appropriate sources for support in promoting equality and valuing diversity

LLUK optional units can be accessed at: www.lluk.org.uk/3081.htm.

The *New overarching professional standards for teachers, tutors and trainers in the Lifelong Learning Sector* LLUK (2007) can be accessed at: www.lluk.org.uk/documents/professional_standards_for_itts_020107.pdf.

APPENDIX 4 CHECKLIST FOR PROMOTING EQUALITY AND DIVERSITY

Identifying needs

- Do your publicity materials contain all the information needed to represent all those for whom it is intended?

- Do you provide information, advice and guidance to help learners choose the right programme, or progress to a relevant programme?

- Is the application and interview process fair to all?

- Are your learners given the opportunity to discuss any additional support requirements, needs, or barriers to learning?

- Do you need to modify the environment, equipment and/or resources in any way, based on these requirements?

- Do your learners have the opportunity to take a learning styles test?

- Can learners take an initial assessment relating to literacy, numeracy, ICT, etc., if relevant?

- Is there a specific initial assessment available in your subject area to help identify a learner's current skills and knowledge?

Planning

- Does your scheme of work reflect the subject in a diverse, yet inclusive way?

- Does your scheme of work build upon topics in a logical way, taking into account any identified needs, and the results of learning styles tests, and initial assessment results?

- Can you provide a choice of learning opportunities at a variety of times and places?

- Does your scheme of work take into account any specialist dates that learners may not be able to attend, or dates that can be celebrated?

- Can you plan time for tutorials – group and individual?

- Does the teaching environment you have been allocated fulfil the needs of your subject and learners; is it safe and accessible?

- Do your session plans take into consideration the individual needs of your learners?

- Can you agree a differentiated individual learning plan with each of your learners?

- Do you use an induction checklist to ensure all aspects of the programme, and the organisation, are stated?

- Is time allocated during induction for information and discussion regarding equality and diversity, including policies, complaints and appeals?

- Can you include a workshop or session regarding equality and diversity, or include specialist speakers?

Designing

- Do your resources represent the diverse range of your learners?

- Do you need to adapt any resources to suit your learners, for example, the use of large print, coloured paper, etc.?

- Do you check all presentations, handouts, etc., to ensure they are legible, and readable by all learners, without using too much jargon?

- Do you need to obtain or arrange for any specialist equipment or support?

Facilitating

- Can you use a suitable inclusive icebreaker?

- Can you agree suitable ground rules with your learners?

- Do you use a variety of stimulating teaching activities, methods and resources to cover all learning styles?

- Do you treat your learners as individuals, using their names when possible?

- Can all learners access the teaching environment, and use all relevant equipment and materials?

- Is your teaching environment conducive to learning, for example, layout, accessibility?

- Is the language you use appropriate and non-discriminatory?

- Do you manage discussions within the learning environment to ensure learner language is appropriate and non-discriminatory?

- Do you ensure individual learner needs are met and differentiate for all abilities?

- Do you take into account all learning styles?

- Do you treat all learners fairly?

- Do you ensure all learners treat each other with respect?

- Can you arrange for any reasonable adjustments to take place if required?

- Do you encourage teamwork?

- Do you present materials and topics in ways that are sensitive to equality and diversity?

- Can you build in sufficient time for group activities to promote communication, bearing in mind any cultural clashes that may occur?

- Is diversity included within your teaching and resources, for example, referring to a variety of cultures, faiths, religions and traditions?

- Are people from diverse backgrounds, for example, cultural, socio-economic, people with disabilities, etc., visible in your resources?

- Can you confidently challenge prejudice and stereotyping between your learners?

- Can you put your own attitudes, values and beliefs behind if they conflict with your learners?

- Do you use appropriate body language and non-verbal communication?

- Do you touch learners in a way that could be construed as inappropriate?

Assessing

- Are appropriate assessment methods used for all learners?

- Is assessment fair and not discriminative against any learner?

- Can you use alternative forms of assessment, for example, reading questions to a learner that is partially sighted?

- Do you need to contact the Awarding/Examining body to obtain extra time for assessments or exams?

- Do you give feedback on an individual basis, giving developmental support where necessary, at a level to suit each learner?

- Can you rephrase questions if they are not understood by the learner?

- Do you differentiate for learners' abilities and needs?

- Are your learners aware of the appeals procedure?

Evaluating

- Do learners have the opportunity to evaluate their programme in an anonymous way?

- Can all learners understand the questions being asked, and complete the necessary forms?

- Do you collect an adequate range of data regarding ethnicity, retention, achievement, progression?

- Do you analyse the data collected and do something positive with it?

- Can you follow up any feedback from learners or others?

- Can you foster links with the local community to improve your own knowledge?

- Can you take any further training to benefit yourself and your learners?

Teacher: **Date:**

Learner: **Venue:**

Issues discussed	
Progress and achievements	
Action required with target dates	

Signed (learner):   Signed (teacher):

APPENDIX 6 PERSONAL DEVELOPMENT PLAN

Name:

Organisation:

Timescale	Aims		Costs involved/ organisational support	Start date	Review date	Completion date CPD record to be updated
Short term						
Medium term						
Long term						

Name:

Organisation:

IfL number:

Date	Activity	Venue	Duration	Justification towards teaching role/subject specialism	Further training needs	Evidence ref number e.g. personal reflections, notes, certificates, etc.

APPENDIX 8 REFLECTIVE LEARNING JOURNAL

Name: **Date:**

Experience *significant event* *or incident*	
Describe *who, what, when, where*	
Analyse *why, how* *(impact on teaching* *and learning)*	
Revise *changes and/or* *improvements* *required*	